Dona Z.

Dat eaving off-loom

01

3634n

DATE			

© THE BAKER & TAYLOR CO.

WEAVING OFF-LOOM

WEAVING OFF-LOOM

DONA Z. MEILACH
AND
LEE ERLIN SNOW

Henry Regnery Company • Chicago

Also by Dona Z. Meilach and Lee Erlin Snow

Creative Stitchery

Other books by Dona Z. Meilach in this series:

Contemporary Leather: Art and Accessories
Creating Art from Anything
Creating Art from Fibers and Fabrics
Creating with Plaster
Creative Carving
The Artist's Eye

Also:

Macramé Accessories
Macramé: Creative Design in Knotting
Making Contemporary Rugs and Wall Hangings
Contemporary Art with Wood
Contemporary Batik and Tie-Dye
Contemporary Stone Sculpture
Papercraft
Papier-Mâché Artistry
Printmaking
Direct Metal Sculpture (with Donald Seiden)
Sculpture Casting (with Dennis Kowal)
Collage and Found Art (with Elvie Ten Hoor)
Accent on Crafts

All photos by Dona and Mel Meilach unless otherwise credited.

Library of Congress Cataloging in Publication Data

Meilach, Dona Z
  Weaving off-loom.

  1. Hand weaving. I. Snow, Lee Erlin, joint author. II. Title.
TT848.M45   746.1'4   72-11198

Published by Henry Regnery Company
180 North Michigan Avenue, Chicago, Illinois 60601
Manufactured in the United States of America
Library of Congress Catalog Card Number: 72-11198
International Standard Book Number: 0-8092-8922-9

ACKNOWLEDGMENTS

The cooperation of hundreds of people is required to bring together the material in a book like this. We wish to express our deepest gratitude to the artists who submitted photos and to those who shipped and brought their work to be photographed. Each artist is credited where his work appears. We wish we could have used all the excellent examples submitted to us, but that would have required a three-volume book.

We are indebted to the professional photographers and to many nonprofessionals who carefully followed photographic suggestions so their work would be presented in the best possible manner. We are especially grateful to Richard Gross, Los Angeles, California, for his splendid photographs of the fiber sculptures taken during the "Deliberate Entanglements" show in Los Angeles. Our thanks, too, to Eudorah Moore, Curator of Design, Pasadena Art Museum, Pasadena, California, and to Bernard Kester, University of California at Los Angeles, for cooperation and permission to use this material.

Gallery directors and curators of museum textile departments were very helpful. Our appreciation to Dorothy Garwood, The Egg and The Eye Gallery, Los Angeles, and Linda Kramer, American Crafts Council, New York, for suggestions of artists to contact. We were privileged to work with acknowledged experts in special areas who demonstrated their techniques: Lydia Van Gelder, Santa Rosa, California, for the section on bobbin lace; Candace Crockett, Woodside, California, for the spinning demonstration; Frances C. Weber, Chattanooga, Tennessee, for her carefully developed ideas for working on round shapes, and Joan Austin, San Diego, California, for the series on basket coiling.

We are delighted to single out the help of Joyce Wexler, Beverly Hills, California, for her cooperation on any and every request, including photographer's assistant, model, and hostess at an exciting off-loom brainstorming session.

Ben Lavitt and Harold Smolin, Astra Photo, Chicago, have our deep gratitude for their expertise and custom photo work, which contributes to the high visual quality of the book. We also want to thank Stan Regula for the drawings and Marilyn Regula for her masterful typing of the final manuscript, both of Morton Grove, Illinois.

Most of all, we must bow to the cooperation of our husbands and children, who managed too well without us during the many hours it took to bring these pages to fruition.

Dona Z. Meilach, Palos Heights, Illinois
Lee Erlin Snow, Los Angeles, California

Dedicated to Mel, Sue, Al, Herb, and Dana

Contents

1 The Meaning of Weaving Off-Loom   2
2 Fibers and Colors and How to Use Them   10
3 Weaves and Ways to Use Them   20
4 Frames and Boards   48
5 Cardboard and Other Devices   66
6 Hoops and Other Objects   78
7 Sculptural Fiber Forms   100
8 Primitive Weaving and Braiding   114
9 Lace As an Off-Loom Technique   122
10 Spinning and Twisting Plies   134
11 Knotless Netting, or Looping   140
12 Crochet   156
13 Basketry Techniques   174
14 Potpourri of Additional Ideas   182

Information Center   196
Selected Bibliography   199
Index   200

1 The Meaning of Weaving Off-Loom

The concept of weaving off-loom is as old as it is new. In a sense, it is just being rediscovered. Ever since the new Stone Age, man has woven fibers to create cloth, and he probably began by using only his fingers. Generally, weaving off-loom refers to hand weaving; mechanical, sophisticated, large looms are not used. The weaving may be accomplished on any object improvised to hold the warp while the weft is passed in and out through the warp with the fingers or with a needle. Some procedures are accomplished only with the fingers.

Objects improvised for weaving off-loom might be the branch of a tree, a frame, or a cardboard shape; these objects are usually small and portable. They bear no resemblance to floor and table harness looms. So, in popular usage, while the improvised item may serve as a loom in that it holds the warp taut, it must be understood that off-loom refers to the simple, almost primitive methods for interlacing fibers to create cloth.

Such weavings do not necessarily adhere to the square, rectangular, or circular shapes we are accustomed to in fabric yardage, in rugs, and in traditional woven wall hangings. They are often freeform and sculptural with great flows of cascading material. The edges may be uneven; the interiors may incorporate negative areas and floating warps.

The fibers used and their combinations are innovative and often startling to an eye accustomed to seeing flat, plain-woven, and pictorial tapestries, rugs, and hangings. The off-loom creation is apt to combine unspun with handspun wools and other natural fibers. It also may utilize some of the hundreds of synthetic fibers now available in scores of textures and colors. Long, flowing fringes and the weaving itself may boast beads, bells, shells, bones, found objects, and an assortment of ingeniously planned baubles

ORIMONO. Momo Nagano. Frame weaving, braiding, knotting. Jute, horsehair, linen, and wool. 4 feet high, 3 feet wide. *Photo, Beth Hazard.*

that are, inevitably, an important and expressive part of the composition. The weaver explores materials and their qualities, and any material is fair game.

Colors and their usage are important aspects of contemporary statements with yarns. Time-tested color theories are often altered innovatively to make a new color statement depending upon how one color fiber reacts with another. Yarn colors can be joined and woven next to each other so that one enhances the other. Of course, yarns do not mix in the same way that pigments are combined by the painter. The result of color placement and the texture of the yarn used must be planned carefully and controlled for a cohesive weaving.

The weaving procedures illustrated are essentially those that have been used for hundreds of years. Examples used throughout the book were carefully analyzed, and many essential weaves adapted to off-loom techniques are shown in the various chapters. These weaves include *plain weave*, or *tabby, twill, twining, lace weaves, rya* and *ghiordes knots, coiling,* and special suggestions for endings, such as braiding, macramé, lace braiding, plying, unplying, and others.

In addition, several techniques, all ancient but updated, are demonstrated because they are part of contemporary fiber statements. These include knotless netting, which has been found in the baskets, carrying bags, and utilitarian items of American Indian tribes and in ancient Egyptian textiles. Finger weaving and Osage braiding, often attributed to American Indians, have no real documented beginning in time. In fact, the same technique often exists in different cultures under various names. Knotless netting, for example, is often called "looping" and "needle lace." Osage braiding, as practiced by the Indians, is another form of finger weaving that shows up in centuries-old textiles from different countries.

Crochet, also illustrated as an off-loom weaving method, is essentially an interlacing of fibers. Crochet pieces are so evident as entire artistic statements and as an adjunct to weaving and knotless netting that crochet techniques had to be included in a comprehensive book on modern off-loom techniques. The examples in the crochet chapter and those projects that use crochet as part of the statement will attest to its validity as an artist's technique.

It is difficult to visualize what is happening with ancient basketmaking methods until you observe the examples in Chapter 13. Baskets, normally associated with utilitarian objects made of grasses such as reeds, raffia, and rattan, are now being created with a wide variety of fibers associated with weaving. Basket shapes formed by *wrapping, twining,* and *coiling* methods that are centuries old are being used to make new statements, and new proponents for creating them are being found. Modern-day baskets may or may not be utilitarian, but certainly they are sculptural and expressive. Other weaving techniques often are used to create baskets, and basket techniques are being added to weavings. It is inevitable that basket statements will be considered sculptural fiber forms in the near future.

The sculptural fiber forms illustrated in Chapter 7 are most impressive. It must be stressed that all these fabrics and the way they are shaped were created without the use of traditional upright and floor weaving looms. All were hand woven, using any method for holding the warp that the artist could devise. Large sculptural weavings require yards and yards of fibers; often they are as heavy as a marble or bronze sculpture. They are as important as any art form in more traditional media. While the composition problems posed by these large sculptural weavings are similar to those posed in traditional weavings, the sculptural forms often present more structural challenges. They must exist and utilize space as any sculpture and incorporate all elements and principles of design.

Chapter 10, on hand spinning, is included for readers who wish to spin their own threads from raw wool, silk, hair, cotton, or other materials. Hand spinning can be used to produce textures and yarns that are not available commercially. In Chapter 10 you also will find methods for working hand-spun and other yarns into multiple plies.

Sketch for a weaving on twigs that will be bound together to make the form. Sketch indicates areas of flat weave and knotted relief techniques. Martha Underwood.

WEAVING ON DRIFTWOOD. Lois Constantine. Free needle-weaving with wool yarns. 12 inches high, 8 inches wide, 10 inches deep.

Working methods are stressed throughout the book. No method represents a rigid technique that must be followed to the letter. Rather, all techniques are offered as ideas for developing procedures that are best for you; they allow you to experiment, to improvise, to take off in any direction. They encourage creativity, mobility, and freedom. And along these lines, photos of objects that can stimulate your own compositions or motifs for weavings are offered. Most artists are aware of the necessity of transposing visual images of their environment into their work. Several photos of scenes and objects, such as those on pages 27, 41, and 44-46, have been chosen that might have stimulated specific works. Use them to stimulate ideas for compositions based on natural or man-made forms. They can spark ideas for shapes to be incorporated in a weaving or for entire weavings. No two artists looking at the same photo make the same visual presentation in a finished piece, so feel free to use them for your individual expression.

Among the benefits of weaving off-loom is that anyone can begin with minimal materials and no equipment other than a branch, yarn, and scissors. You also can weave only with paper. The projects and methods illustrated are adaptable to literally every age level—beginning with young children and advancing to the most sophisticated weaver.

ROCKS. Earlene Ahrens. Any object can be warped; then it can be woven around.

TOPOGRAPHY. Sandra Koerlin. 6 inches high, 10 inches wide, 15 inches long. Woven linen on a fruit crate suggests a topographical view of a surface. Weaving and crate combine as a finished object. A box could also be used for the weaving frame from which the weaving could be removed. *Courtesy, Artist.*

PAPER WEAVING. The principle of weaving can be easily accomplished with paper. Colors with plain weave can create great visual movement.

Twigs bound together by yarns form an interesting shape into which weaving can be accomplished.

WEAVING ON WOOD. Lee Erlin Snow. 10 inches high, 40 inches long. The finished woven twigs are combined with feathers and beads. Only a long needle with a large eye was used for weaving the wool yarns.

EINO'S BRANCH. Momo Nagano.
24 inches high, 20 inches wide.
Linen weaving on a found branch
using plain and open weaves.

HANGING (detail). Virginia Black.
Weaving concepts today are often
loose and freely shaped. They
combine many weave patterns in
one composition and utilize a
variety of fibers and objects.

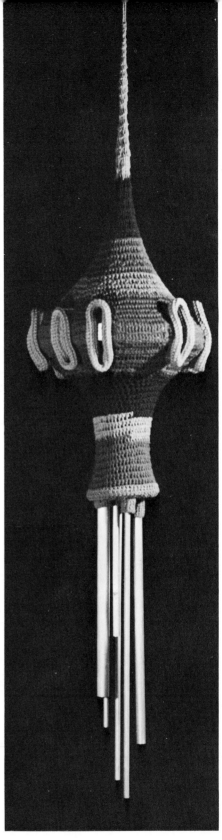

CROCHETED HANGING. Jane
Knight. Three-dimensional objects
are popular in off-loom techniques,
whether they are crocheted, woven
or designed by a combination of
many techniques. *Photo, Richard
Knight.*

FEATHERED FUNGUS. Lucele
Coutts. Traditional basketweaving
and coiling techniques are worked
into a contemporary shape often
resembling baskets but moving
toward a sculptural statement. This
coiled basket, made of rug wool
and knitting worsted on a fiber rush
coil, also incorporates rya knotting.

2 Fibers and Colors and How to Use Them

Fibers are the raw material of the weaver, and there are as many approaches to using them as there are craftsmen. Looking at bins of assorted weaving threads and ropes in a myriad of natural and man-made fibers can stimulate color and design ideas. Generally, weavers buy many skeins, hanks, or cones of yarn and keep them on hand ready for use. Some weavers work from a sketch and then buy the material they need for a particular presentation. Often a commission or specific project determines how the work will proceed.

The weaver must learn about fibers. He must experiment with materials and blends to test their mobility and obtain the textures and visual appeal he seeks. A familiarity with fibers results from a gradual learning process: searching out new materials, buying some, experimenting, accepting, and rejecting. Writing for sample cards from the supply sources given in the Appendix is a quick way to gain a broad knowledge of the types of available materials. Many specialty yarns are not available through usual retail yarn and department stores. Today there are so many fibers on the market that it is helpful to categorize them by content and type.

Animal Fibers

These include threads made from the fur and hair of animals, such as wool from sheep, alpaca from llamas, yakhair from yaks, mohair from goats, camel's hair from camels, silk from silkworms, and so forth. Fleece refers to the coat of wool that covers a sheep or other animal. When fleece is carded and pulled into lengths preparatory to spinning, it is called "roving."

Wool fibers are available in a vast variety, from very thin,

ERUPTIONS (detail). Tadek Beutlich. *Courtesy, "Deliberate Entanglements," UCLA.*

single-ply strands to thick three- and four-ply yarns. Wool fibers from various countries differ greatly, depending on the animals, climate, and certain environmental conditions (see Chapter 10 on spinning).

Vegetable Fibers

Fibers derived from plants are considered vegetable fibers. Cotton from the cotton shrub is probably the most plentiful and is available in a wide assortment. Linen from the flax plant varies greatly in quality and textures available and is more popular than cotton for hand weaving.

Jute from the jute plant and hemp from the hemp plant, which are both made into coarse and fine fibers, are associated with burlap, rope, twine, and warm, earth shades of browns and beiges. Suppliers now dye them many attractive colors (not all colorfast), which can add interest to weavings. These fibers are strong and are available in several different ply and in diameters up to about one inch.

Sisal and henequen are derived from agave plants. Like jute and hemp, they are used for twines and ropes but are usually coarser and stiffer than jute and hemp fibers. Sisal and henequen tend to be scratchy, so wear gloves to facilitate working with them.

Synthetic — or Man-Made — Fibers

The variety of synthetic fibers available is incredible. Since man learned to create fibers from chemical compounds, an entire new industry has developed. Rayon, one of the first synthetic fibers produced, was created as a substitute for silk. Other synthetic fibers that you will discover when checking labels are Nylon, Dynel, Orlon, Acrylic, and Orlon-Acrylic. Various blends of synthetic materials are available. Some of the strongest and most attractive fibers are blends of animal and vegetable yarns or blends of synthetic with animal and vegetable yarns. A heavy rug yarn, for example, may be composed of rayon and cotton or wool and nylon.

Other Varieties

As you search for threads, yarns, ropes, and twines, you'll discover infinite exciting combinations that yield a great variety of appearances, colors, textures, and strengths. Some of these varieties may be labeled as:

Plain yarn—those with straight strands that are evenly twisted or braided.

Novelty yarns—those nubby varieties with little bumps and an uneven surface.

Looped yarns—those with thin and thick spirals and tiny, tight twists that appear along a basic thread.

Different distributors and/or manufacturers refer to yarns by various names, so always ask for samples before ordering.

Raffia, palm leaves, plastic tubing, thin silver and gold wire, rubber-covered wire, monofilament twine, baler's twine, leather, and suede strips are among the materials used in many weavings throughout the book. These materials are not usually associated with the weaver's art, but the modern approach to weaving is that any material can be used that contributes to the total visual and tactile quality of the work.

Fibers applied to wall hangings and other art forms may be more varied and randomly used than those woven into fabrics for clothing and furniture. The purpose and weight of clothing fabric must be considered. Given the rich texture of most wools, it is often a temptation to weave heavy fabrics that may be impractical for sewing into garments. The same is true when considering materials for draperies and furnishings; these should be durable but not so stiff or textured that they will not hang or wear properly.

Count and Ply

When a fiber is spun, it is formed into a continuous thread of a certain size and strength. The finished thread is given a standardized number based on the amount of yarn required to make a pound. This number is referred to as the *count*, and it designates the size of, or thickness of, the thread. A fine thread will have more length per pound and a higher number than a heavy, coarse yarn. For instance, a no. 1 is a coarse-count thread with 840 yards per pound. A no. 20 thread will be very fine and have 20×840 yards, or 16,800 yards per pound. There is no standardization for novelty yarns as the thread design determines the weight and length.

A strand of yarn is called a *single*. When two or more single strands are twisted together, they form a "ply." Most weaving yarns are twisted into 2 ply, 3 ply, 4 ply, etc. Rope, such as jute, hemp, and sisal, may be woven into as many as 8 or 10 ply. When a thread is marked, for example, as 20/2, it means that it is a no. 20 count thread in a 2 ply. Nylon is often braided rather than twisted. All threads with multiple ply can be untwisted to make attractive endings or to create textures within a weaving.

Estimating Quantities Needed

Weaving yarns generally are sold by weight, such as ½ ounce, 2 ounces, 4 ounces, 8 ounces, 1 pound, etc. and are packaged

Fiber samples are available from sources listed in the Appendix. Keep them filed or organized in a notebook for ready reference.

in balls, skeins, tubes, and cones. Estimating amounts required is often "iffy," but you can predetermine a general idea of how much you will need for a particular project by a simple procedure.

For example, begin with a known weight of yarn, such as 5 ounces of handspun wool. Work up a sample square in the average density of the weave desired. Then,

1. Multiply the length by the width of the sampler.
2. Weigh the sampler on a postage, diet, or kitchen scale. (Heavy ropes can be weighed on a bathroom scale.)
3. Multiply the height by the width of the frame, board, or finished size you want the weaving to be to find the number of square inches in the finished piece.

Then use this formula: $\dfrac{\text{sq. in. of sampler}}{\text{wt. of sampler}} = \dfrac{\text{total sq. in.}}{x \text{ (total wt. needed)}}$

For example, assume you begin with 5-ounce skein, and the sampler is 4 inches by 4 inches:

1. 4 × 4   = 16 square inches
2. The weight of the sampler   = 1 ounce
3. The frame size measures 12 inches by 20 inches   = 240 square inches
4. Amount of yarn needed   = x

Then:

$\dfrac{16}{1} = \dfrac{240}{x}$ or 16 x = 240; then divide 240 by 16 = 15 ounces.

You now know that you would need three 5-ounce skeins of yarn to make your project.

Always allow extra yarn for warp and additional endings or headings. Always buy a little more than you need, and all at one time, to assure a uniform dye lot.

When using different colors, figure the amount of each color you will need by weights also, such as 4 ounces red, 2 ounces white, 1 ounce black.

Sometimes it is necessary to work with yardage rather than weight; then the following conversion table can be applied.

Fiber	Count No.	Yards per Pound
Cotton	1	840
	2	1,680
Wool (unplied)	1	1,600
Worsted wool (plied)	1	560
	2	1,120
Linen	1	300
Spun silk	1	840

Color

Color is an exciting, often frustrating, but crucial aspect of weaving. The beginner is advised to adhere to simple one-, two-, and three-color schemes until he learns how combined colors and textures react.

There are shortcuts to using color effectively in your work. One technique is to apply color wheel principles and other color theories. Another is to study a painting and adapt its color relationships and proportions to a weaving. For example, a painting may be composed of only three colors with different tones and values of those colors used in unequal proportions. You can adapt the same colors and proportions for fibers that you would use in a painting.

Nature offers limitless ideas for color schemes. Earth-tones, such as browns, rusts, ochers, and golds, used together can produce subtle colorings that are almost always successful. The colors and their distributions found in one rose, one petunia, a leaf, or in algae on a rock can be adapted to color schemes in a weaving. For example, open a green pepper and study the many nuances of green; hold it up to the light to see how different it looks when shadows fall upon it. Then try to match the greens in yarns. These ready-made sources for color ideas are all around you.

Do the same kind of color analysis with a nasturtium or other live flower. How many colors are there in the stamen, the petals, or the stem that contribute to make up the whole? Which color dominates? Which color appears in the smallest amount? Use the same colors and distribution for your own compositions.

Before you begin a project, place the skeins or cones of yarns you are planning to work with together to determine how they go with one another and let your eye be the judge. Just because you think yellow, orange, and red should go together, you might find that a particular red is too coral and may not look good next to a light orange. If the values are too similar, they may cancel rather than complement one another.

Dyeing Yarns

Yarns are readily available in scores of colors, values, and shades. Yet there is the possibility that you will not find exactly the shade you want in the yarn you like. You can dye your own yarns using vegetable or synthetic dyes. You also can achieve variegated and tie-dye effects by dyeing only portions of a skein of yarn. You also may bleach out some of the original color for more subtle hues.

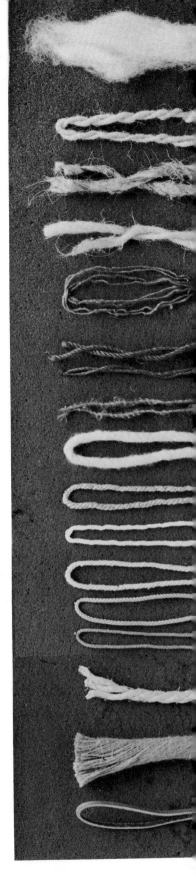

A sampling of fibers used in weavings include (top to bottom): fleece, handspun wool, cotton and linen yarns in plain and novelty strands, sisal, jute, and rawhide.

15

There are several excellent books on natural dye plants, which is a study in itself. The fiber reactive synthetic dyes for cold water dyeing, which are now available at craft shops and from weaving suppliers, are especially good for dyeing natural fibers. These dyes yield brilliant, relatively fade-resistant colors when they are used according to directions. Dyeing yarns is most easily accomplished when the yarns are loosely wound into skeins and tied in a few places to prevent tangling. Those who spin their own fibers are often anxious to dye them as well (see Chapter 10 on spinning).

When dyeing yarns, wind yarn in skeins and tie loose in two or more places to prevent strands from tangling when moved about in the dyebath.

The Color Wheel

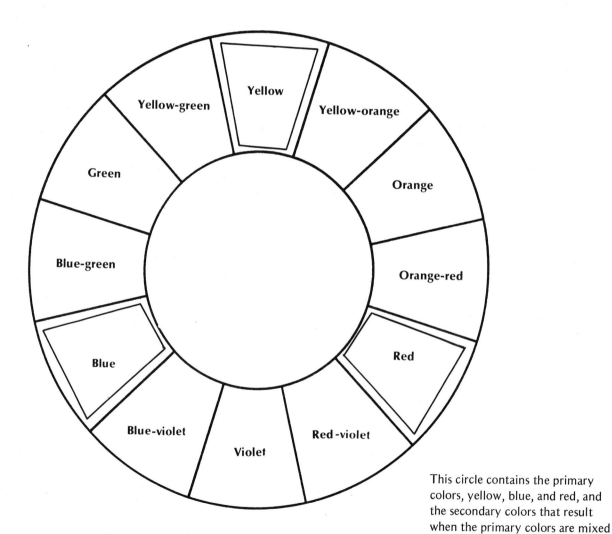

This circle contains the primary colors, yellow, blue, and red, and the secondary colors that result when the primary colors are mixed together.

The color wheel is a popular aid for successfully combining colors, and its principles can be readily applied to fibers. The color wheel is divided into three *primary* colors—yellow, blue, and red. Mixing them with one another yields the *secondary* colors. For example:

$$
\begin{array}{lclcl}
\text{yellow} & + & \text{blue} & = & \text{greens} \\
\text{yellow} & + & \text{red} & = & \text{oranges} \\
\text{blue} & + & \text{red} & = & \text{violets}
\end{array}
$$

Weaving threads are usually already dyed in these primary and secondary colors, but knowing which primary colors mix well will help you develop your own color schemes. If you buy a skein of blue-green thread, you will understand that a primary bright blue and a bright yellow should blend well. Thread colors used next to one another will create the effect that the Impressionists produced in their paintings: the eye of the observer will mix the color.

The color wheel also shows complementary colors: those that are opposite each other on the color wheel, such as yellow and violet. When complementary colors are placed next to each other in weaving, they can intensify each other. Other complementary colors are red and green, orange and blue.

Near-complementary colors may be coupled advantageously. These can be determined by referring to the colors on each side of the complementary colors. Combine yellow with blue violet and red violet because these colors lie nearly opposite one another on the color wheel.

Monochromatic schemes (mono means one, chroma means color) use variations of one tone. Experience will show that the highest intensity of color results when the warp and weft are the same or closely related colors. When the warp is slightly lighter or darker than the weft, a more subtle effect is achieved.

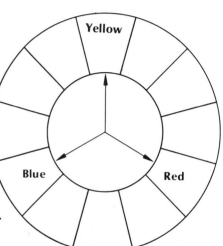

A triad consists of three colors spaced equal distances apart. Any three go well together, such as yellow-red-blue.

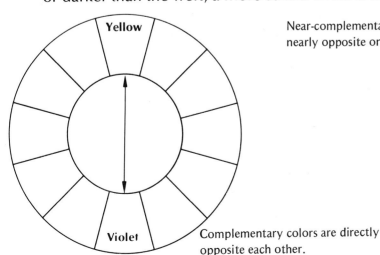

Complementary colors are directly opposite each other.

Near-complementary colors lie nearly opposite one another.

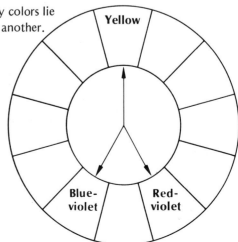

WEAVING OFF-LOOM

Many kinds of fibers are combined for interplays of texture and color. You will find yarns that are smooth, fuzzy, hard, soft, stretchy, and unyielding. You can also employ feathers, metal, ceramics, found objects, and anything that you feel will fit into the composition. Wires, rubber, and plastic cords may be successfully used.

TO KEEP IS TO BE KEPT. Walter Nottingham. Wool. Free warp weaving with wrapping and photoemulsion. *Courtesy, Artist.*

Details (left to right): Linda Borlund, Dorothy Riley, Suellen Glashausser.

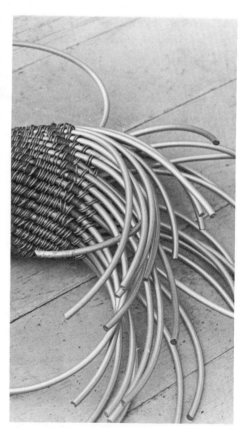

WEAVING (detail). Martha Underwood. 25 inches high, 14 inches wide. Handspun yarns and a variety of wools.

MY THING #1 (detail). Stephanie Cyr. Hanging made with 1/2- and 1-inch strips of fabric and beads. Full piece is 6 feet long. *Courtesy, Artist.*

3 Weaves and Ways to Use Them

The weaving process consists of interlacing weft threads under and over warp threads. No matter how complex or simple the weaving is, the procedure is basically the same: yarn is strung back and forth in parallels across a space or board. This original stringing is called the *warp*. The yarn that is woven under and over the warp is called the *weft*. The manner in which the weft is interlaced with the warp is the *weaving pattern*. And that's where the fun begins.

The modern approach to weaving uses traditional and non-traditional weaves in infinite combinations. Once you have worked a weave, it is part of your weaving vocabulary, and you are free to change and experiment with it as your artistic taste dictates. Weaves may be called by different names in various books. The names and numbers of weaves you know are not as important as how you combine them with one another and with the textures and colors of the threads you select. The raw materials of the weaver can make a dramatic statement when creatively used.

The weaves illustrated throughout the book offer more than basic information. They represent designs used in the majority of pieces throughout the book. One could work indefinitely by combining only the demonstrated weaves. However, you can explore literally hundreds of weaves in scores of excellent books, some of which are listed in the Bibliography. Weaves planned for looms also can be interpreted in off-loom weaving methods.

Weaving a Sampler

The beginning weaver can experiment with the weaves by working them on a piece of rigid cardboard about 10 inches by 12 inches. The top and bottom edges should be notched at about ½-inch intervals to hold the warp. Use a nonstretchy rug or

Materials required for weaving are minimal. You need a surface to hold the weaving, a comb-like toothed instrument for "beating," or pushing, the weft into place. These can be a special beater carved from wood, a comb, or a fork. For weaving the weft you can use a yarn needle, a steel tapestry needle, or any large-eye pointed instrument that will carry the weft.

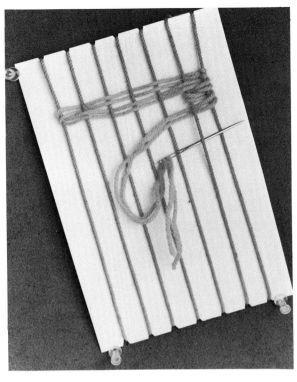

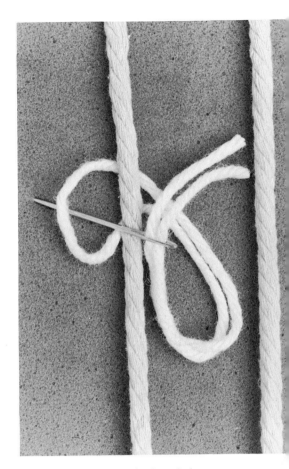

The series of vertical parallel threads that is the basis for weaving is called the *warp*. The threads that are interlaced horizontally under and over the warp are called the *weft*. A piece of notched cardboard can be warped and used for practicing the patterns and for creating an entire weaving.

Yarns can be double-threaded through the needle and worked as two wefts at once.

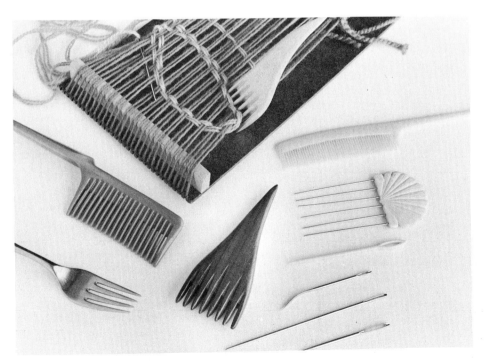

weaving yarn and tape it at the back of the cardboard; then warp the yarn around the cardboard into the notches as shown at left. Warp cords placed close together will result in a tight weave; those that are spaced far apart will yield an open weave. As you weave, you will see how different patterns either cover or expose the warp for various design effects.

Warp cords should be wound so that they create tension but still allow a little "give." They should be close enough together to hold the weft in place after it is "beaten" up. *Beating* means that you push the weft into place with a special beater tool or with an improvised tool, such as a fork, comb, or hair teaser.

The warp tightens as the weaving progresses. If it is wound too tight to begin with, the weaving may curl or buckle. If the warp is too loose, the weaving will be uneven and the threads will shift from their planned position.

To begin weaving, thread one end of about a 3-foot-long weft through a large-eye needle leaving a 3-inch tail that can be woven into the back later. Tie the other end around the first warp. Proceed by passing the weft *under* the second warp, *over* the third, *under* the fourth, *over* the fifth, and so on, all across the first row. Use your needle to pick over and under the warp. Then alternate the second row going *over* the warp you went *under* in the first row. This simple over-one, under-one pattern is the foundation of weaving and is referred to as *plain* or *tabby weave*.

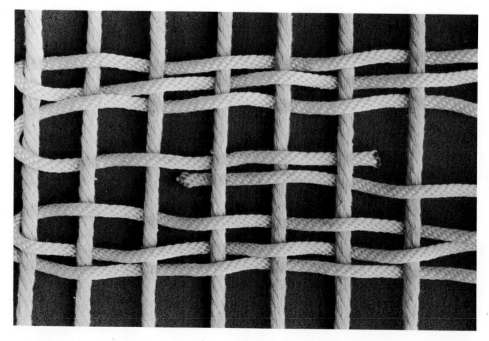

To add a new length of cord of the same color, lay the new length directly beneath the old one and weave them together for an inch or two. Then beat all the yarns together, including the next row above and below. Allow loose ends to fall to the back so that they can be woven in later with a crochet hook or snipped off (or two threads can be knotted together at the back of the weaving).

To avoid weaving too tight, which causes distortion to the side edges, pass the weft loosely across the warp in an arch—this is called *bubbling*—so that the yarn actually is a little longer than necessary for the row. Then use your beater and push the yarn up to meet the preceding row. Both bubbling and beating the yarn into place are conventional weaving methods regardless of the loom used. When your weft runs out anywhere in the weaving, place a new weft below it in the same weave pattern for about 1 inch and continue to weave, allowing the loose ends of the old and new weft to fall to the back of the weaving, where they can be woven in or snipped off later. Then weave the next row and beat the threads up so the joining will be lost in the weaving.

To simplify the weaving procedure, you can separate the warps by weaving a narrow, flat stick such as a ruler, tongue depressor, or one-inch-wide strip of cardboard across the warps. This object is called a *shed stick* because it keeps open the space between the warps—the *shed*. The shed stick holds the warps apart so you can quickly pass the weft in and out, working in one direction; the shed stick is then flattened and the needle is used to pick over and under the warp in the opposite direction. For the next row, lifting the shed stick opens the shed so you can pass the weft through again. As you weave, avoid splitting the warp threads or crossing them over. In Chapter 4 additional methods for holding the shed open with heddles are described.

The *shed* is the opening between the warps through which the weft is passed. To make weaving easier a stick is placed between the warps so that the needle can be passed through. For weaving the next row, the shed stick is flattened, and the needle is used to pick the over-under weave.

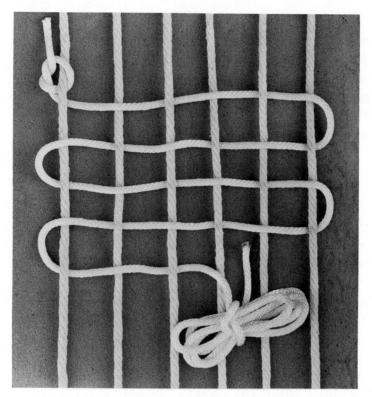

Plain weave, or *tabby,* is the foundation of weaving. To begin, tie the weft to the first warp and proceed under one and over one. For the second row, alternate and go over the cord that you went under in the first row. Then alternate each row. Weaving with cords that will not fit through a needle's eye can be done by winding the yarn into a butterfly and passing it through the warps by hand.

Under two, over two is a variation of plain weave. You pass the weft under two, then over two; alternate in the second row by going over the two you went under in the first row and under the two you went over in the previous row. In these weaves vertical stripes are created by using two or more color wefts in separate needles.

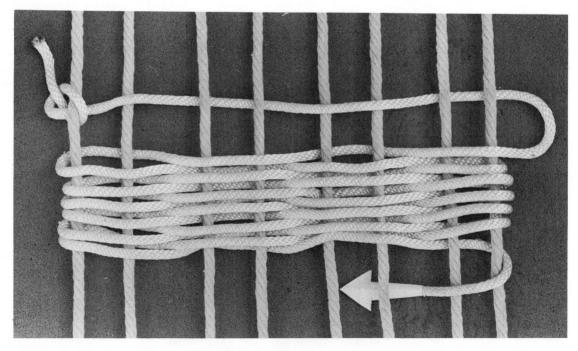

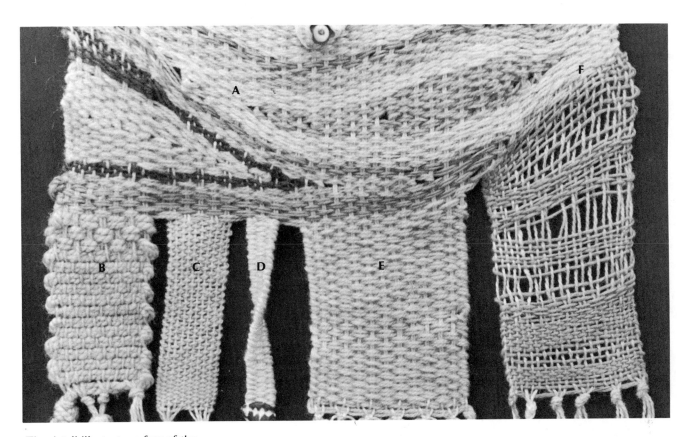

The detail illustrates a few of the
countless design variations possible
using only tabby and under two,
over two weaves in different ways.
A) Plain weave or tabby can be
shaped by beating the weft in an
interesting line and filling other
threads in and around that line.
B) Tabby with 2 threads used in the
needle simultaneously. C) Tabby.
D) Under two, over two tightly
woven and packed down with the
beater. E) Under two, over two
with two threads, as in B.
F) Loosely woven tabby alternated
with shaped weft and tightly woven
tabby. Lee Erlin Snow.

HANGING. Sharon Jaunsem. 50 inches high, 36 inches wide. The slit tapestry technique is cleverly adapted in different areas of the weaving. The many textures, colors, and weave patterns help to accentuate the differences in the panels. The oval relief shape is made with the rya knot, described on page 29.

Dovetailing and slit techniques on angles can be used in one composition.

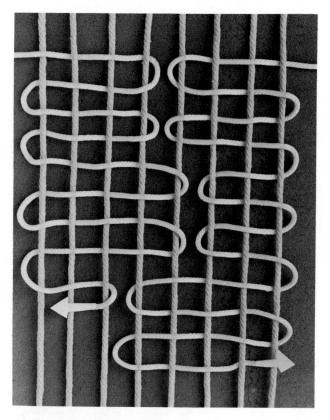

Slit tapestry weave is used to create color changes within a weft row. It is also used to separate panels and to create negative areas within a work. Study the demonstration carefully and observe that adjacent wefts maintain the weaving pattern on each side of the slit. When slits are made using the same colors, you will require two weft cords—one to weave with on each side of the panel.

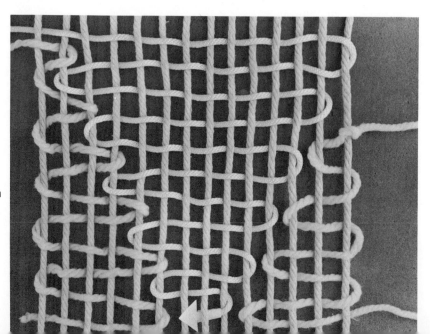

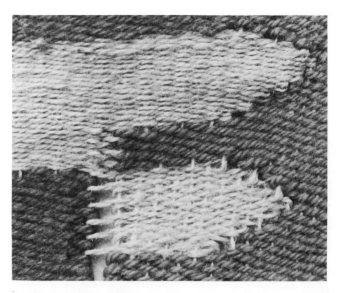

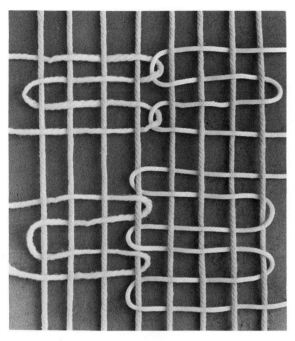

Dovetailing and interlocking are used to effect the color change. Detail, Momo Nagano.

Interlocking and dovetailing are techniques for changing thread and textures while keeping the warps together. To interlock (top) pass two weft colors from each side and loop them around each other between a warp, as shown. When interlocking the wefts, continue in one weft row to effect a color change in that row.

To dovetail (bottom) each color shares a warp, and one cord is higher than the other. Dovetail can be used for horizontal weaving and for filling in odd shapes. Gradual diagonals and straight-edge color changes can be accomplished with these weaves depending upon the placement of the wefts on the different warps.

Directions of color changes within a weaving can be suggested by many forms. The design of this modern hotel in Tunisia, North Africa, can suggest straight and diagonal color areas and shapes for a weaving pattern.

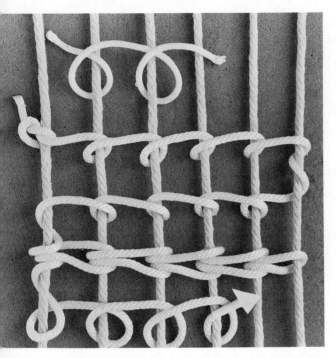

THE TEXTURE KNOTS

Soumak is considered a "wrapped warp" technique because in this procedure the weft actually encircles each warp; no shed is used. The weft passes over the warp and loops behind it and over itself in front. Soumak, originally a rug knotting method, is effectively used as a detail and a contrast to tabby. It is especially sturdy when held between rows of tabby. When the knotted rows are separated, one appearance results; when they are beaten close together, the weave resembles the stem stitch in embroidery. If one row of soumak is alternated with one row of tabby, the weave will lie in one direction. Vary the appearance by taking up different combinations of warps. A soft, stretchy yarn will appear flat and linear; a stiff yarn will result in a raised effect.

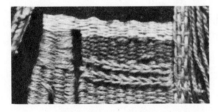

Soumak (detail).

The Egyptian knot is the opposite of the soumak and appears as loops over each warp. The weft is passed under the warp and looped over the front, and it crosses itself behind the warp. Use it as rows of loops or vary it by combining it with tabby and other weaves. A detail of the Egyptian knot can create a distinct motif within a weaving.

EGYPTIAN KNOT (detail). Nadine Shubin.

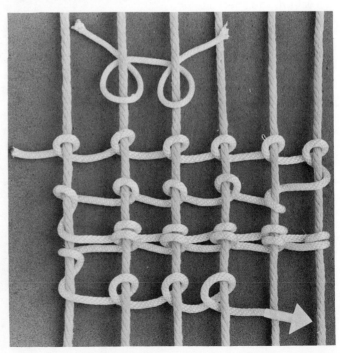

The rya knot (below) uses a continual length of weft cord wrapped about the warp in the same way as the ghiordes. The result is a looped pile rather than cut ends. The length of the loop is controlled by placing a stick or piece of heavy cardboard under the loop as you pass it over and between the warps. Tabby rows hold the loops in place. Surfaces can incorporate various heights of pile or a mixture of loops and cut pile. The loops can be clipped for a cut pile.

The ghiordes and rya knots are rug-knotting techniques that are easily and beautifully adapted to weaving off-loom. They result in a rich raised surface pile. The ghiordes knot (left) is made with cut lengths of yarn. Each length is placed over two warps, and the ends are brought behind, between, and then on top of the warps, as shown. The cut ends form the pile. Rows of tabby hold them in place. The pile can be very long or short; very long yarns can be threaded with beads, bells, buttons, shells, and other objects.

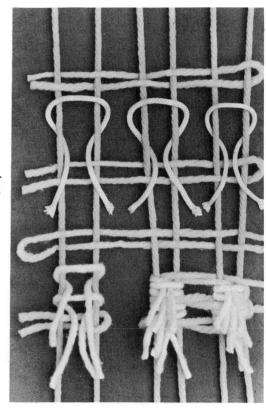

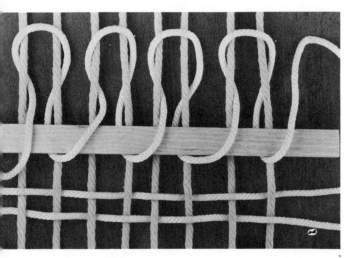

Knots made over a ruler or stick with a continuous weft result in the looped pile of the rya knot.

The looped pile of the rya knot in bulky cotton yarn is combined with the shag, or cut, pile of the ghiordes knot in handspun wool. Both knots yield a raised surface, which contrasts to the flat tabby in yarn and leather strips and to the sections of wrapped warp. Detail, Sharon Jaunsem.

OPEN WEAVES

A variety of airy, open effects can be created within a solid portion of a weaving or as a loose-woven pattern throughout. Many traditional patterns, called by a number of different names, can be used and altered as your own creativity dictates. A few are offered as ideas for digressing from the usual weaves and as a challenge for the more adventurous weaver.

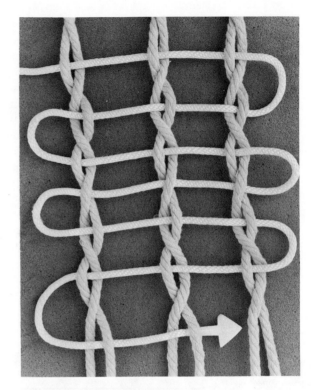

Leno weave, which can result in a casement-type weave, is also called *gauze.* In this weave two or more warp threads are twisted around each other and held by a weft passing through the twist. Twisting the warps tends to shorten them, so you should allow ample length in the warp for loosening tension as necessary.

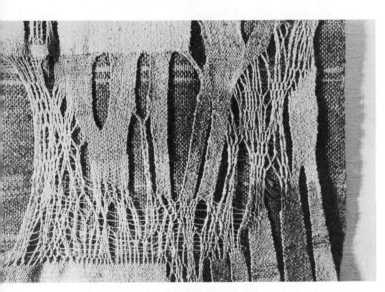

YELLOW FORESTS (detail). Ruth Ginsberg. Areas of leno with the twisted warp and open weft passing through the twist with tabby and slit weaves. *Courtesy, Art Institute of Chicago.*

IT (detail). Marianne Rodwell. Long areas of multiple warps can be twisted in the leno weave and held with a twined weft or two rows of tabby.

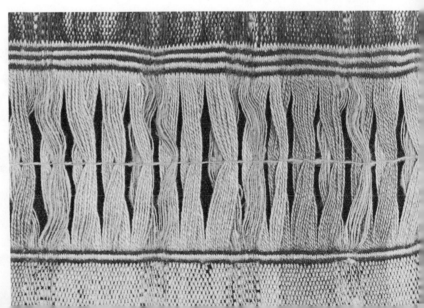

Brooks Bouquet is an open, lacy weave pattern. It can be easily varied by changing the groupings of warp that are wrapped with the weft. The procedure is much like wrapping flower stems—hence its name *Bouquet*. Loop the weft around multiples of warp; each group of warps should be tied tightly with the loop to hold it. These can be spaced and alternated with tabby rows.

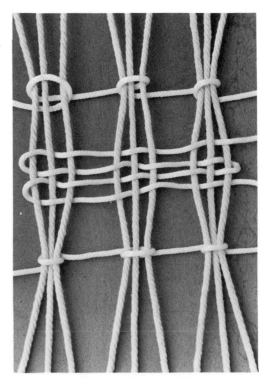

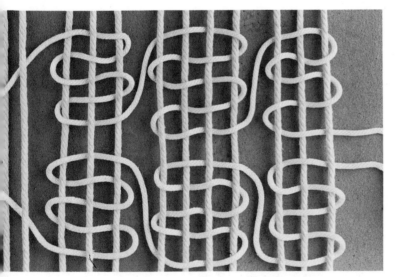

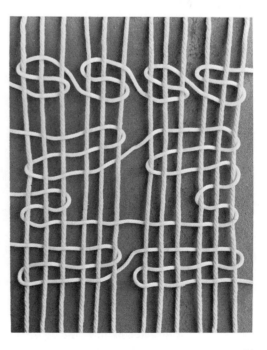

Spanish lace is an open weave that can combine a variety of weft directions over any number of warps. Above is a traditional grouping and arrangement for Spanish lace. At right is one of countless varieties possible that may be coordinated with slit, tabby, and other weaves. Weft colors can be alternated in all these weaves. The warp colors can contribute to pattern too, since they are not completely covered.

OTHER WEAVE IDEAS

Not too many years ago weavings
were composed essentially of
traditional patterns in straight,
unbroken weft rows. Today,
free-form shapes in many colors
and weaves are popular. Wefts are
woven across the warp and pushed
into a desired shape with the beater.
Areas in and around the shape are
filled in to emphasize the shape
with various weaves, colors, and
textures of yarns.

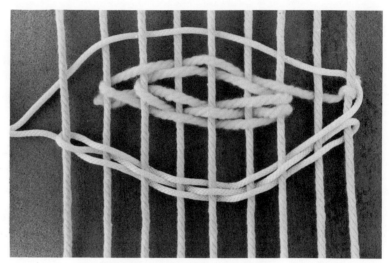

A free-form shape in one yarn can
be filled in with another type and
color of yarn.

An oval shape filled in with rya
knots is a contrast to the flat tabby.

Ideas for shapes and how to fill
them in and the possible use of
ghiordes knot outlining can be
inspired by this close-up from the
bark of a palm tree.

CHILKAT. Lee Erlin Snow. 18
inches high, 12 inches wide. A
variety of free shapes with basic
weaving patterns.

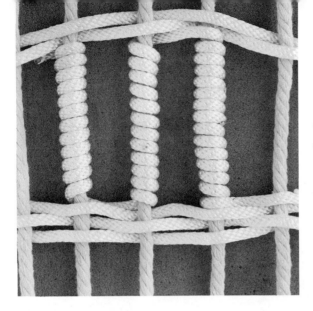

Wrapping the warp. Unwoven, exposed warps often create negative areas and spaces within a weaving. However, in long, open expanses the warps can be wrapped to create greater design interest and to carry through weft colors and textures. Warps can be wrapped individually or as multiples, depending upon the design and closeness of the warp. In double-weave patterns (in which the weaving consists of two layers) top warps are often wrapped in bundles to reveal the weaving beneath. Wrapping consists of winding a thread around the warp. (See wrapping for endings, pages 36-37.)

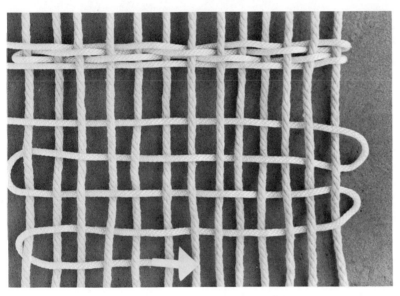

TWILL

The twill weave is often used in loom weaving for tight-woven upholstery and clothing yardage. It can be transposed easily to off-loom weaving to result in a series of staggered diagonal wefts. It does require concentration at first to achieve the correct progression of the diagonal.

Twill lines may run from left to right and from right to left for herringbone patterns, arrows, and zigzags.

Illustrated is a twill that uses the over two, under two weave with each row staggered. It works best when an odd number of warps is used. For row 1, pass the weft over two and under two with only one over at the end. For row 2, move the weft so that it is staggered, as shown, and there are two cords *under* at the row's end. For row 3, stagger the weft over one more warp; end with one over and one under. To continue the diagonal twill, row 4 repeats row 1, row 5 repeats row 2, row 6 repeats row 3, etc. To reverse the twill for a herringbone, stagger the diagonal weft in the opposite direction.

Patterns on a seashell may suggest a design for the twill weave.

COPTIC. Pat Obye. 15 inches high, 12 inches wide. Wrapped warps and woven narrow areas using the slit are combined to achieve negative spaces within the weaving. Observe how different multiples of warp are combined. The tuft at top is the cut pile of the ghiordes knot.

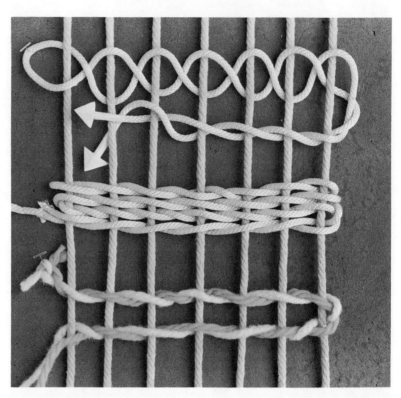

Twining differs from straight weaving in that *two* wefts are simultaneously worked across the warps. One weft is passed over the warp, and one weft is passed under the same warp. The wefts are then crossed, and they change positions over the next warp. Each warp is covered in progression. No shed is required. Once you get the knack of twining, it is easy. Place the wefts under and over the warp, cross them, and turn them over before going to the next warp. This tightly woven, sturdy system is often used for basketweaving.

The pairs of wefts can be the same color or different colors. Variations are accomplished by spacing the twining so that some of the warps show, by double twisting the wefts between each warp, by twining over two warps at a time, or in any manner you can develop.

TWINED HANGING. Kathy Malec. 40 inches high with fringe, 8 inches in diameter. Twining used for the body is worked in the round, starting from under the square knot strips. Plastic hoops hold the circular shape. Wrapping and beads complete the ends.

HANGING (detail). Virginia Black. Sisal, manila, hemp, wheat, and other natural fibers are woven by many different methods, including twining, tabby, under two, over two, and open weaves.

ENDING AND FINISHING
When you finish a weaving, the warp is cut at the back. Allow ample lengths at top and bottom for finishing. Ends should be finished attractively and in such a way so as to relate to the weaving. Examples of endings throughout the book include braiding, woven narrow panels, lace weaving, knotting, wrapping, tassels, beads, metal objects, fur, feathers, leather, and shells. You may also tease the ends or unravel the plies. There is no best way to end a work; the treatment allows room for great variety. Endings may be straight across, curved, angled, or jagged. Headings can be planned to integrate with the bottom while serving as hanging devices to be placed over rods, twigs, washers, and other items for hanging. Loose ends of added cords at the back of the weaving can be tucked into the weave with a needle or a crochet hook and snipped.

Endings include narrow woven strips, wrapping, square and over-hand knots, beads, and a twig. Detail, Martha Underwood.

To wrap with a needle, use one of the warp threads for wrapping over others or introduce a new color or texture as the wrapping thread. A) The finished wrapped threads. B) Begin at the *bottom* of the wrap and overlap the first turn to prevent the coil from slipping. Continue winding. C) Wrap a large-eye needle into the coil with the eye at the top. When you have the desired number of wraps, put the end of the thread through the needle eye. D) Pull the needle through all wraps to the bottom. Tighten the wrap by twisting gently. Remove the needle and trim the thread ends. A dab of glue can be added to the thread ends for extra security.

The *Peruvian wrap* is practical for using cords that are too thick to fit through a needle, for winding different-colored cords, and for wrapping when you do not have a needle. A) Lay out the strand to be wrapped. Place the left end of the cord in a U shape parallel to the strands; bring the right end over, around, and under the strands and under the U shape, as shown.

B) Continue to wind the strands tight until you are near the bottom of the U. (The demonstration cords are loose, but they should be wound tight.) On the last wind, bring the right end through the U and hold with a finger. Pull the left end up and release your finger. The right end will travel up with the pull to tighten the wrap.

Long wrapped endings can be achieved in either of the methods shown or by winding double or triple threads around the base threads and securing them with a needle, as in needle wrapping. Detail, Lee Erlin Snow.

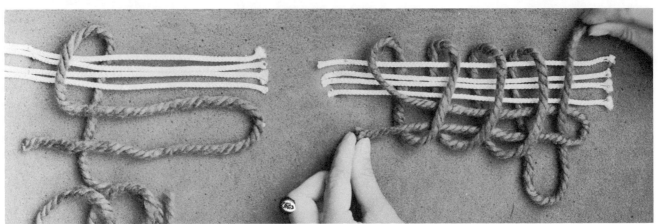

The square knot is an efficient ending method. It is usually made with four cords. The two outside cords are knotted over the two central anchor cords. Bring the right cord over the anchor cords. Place the left cord over the right cord.

Bring the left cord behind the two anchor cords and, from under, bring it through the loop made by the right cord.

Pull evenly for the first half of the square knot.

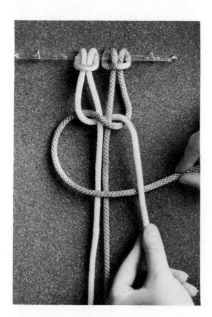

For the second half of the square knot, follow the same procedure but on the right side of the anchor cords. Bring the left cord over the two central anchor cords. Place the right cord over the left.

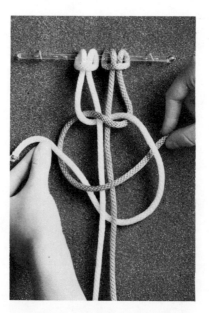

Bring the right cord behind the two anchors and, from behind, bring it through the loop formed by the left cord.

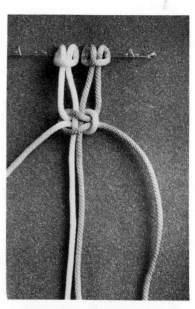

Pull the cords tight. The finished knot will look like this.

WHITE ON WHITE. Sharon
Jaunsem. 60 inches high, 20 inches
wide. Simple braiding and
wrapping. Grouping of threads is
used for endings.

Detail of endings on a weaving.
Sharon Jaunsem. Various materials
are combined with wrapping,
braiding, knotting, beads, and
washers.

Tassels are an excellent adjunct to weaving. They are especially effective for endings.

A woven saddle bag from Bethlehem is decorated with tassels. *Collection, Lee Erlin Snow.*

WEAVING (detail). Phyllis Hall. Tassels are added for ending interest. *Photo, Clement Hall.*

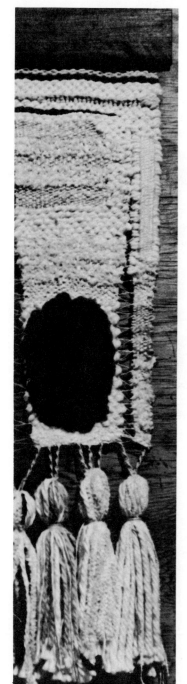

Sketch for a weaving by Martha Underwood suggests tassels and wrappings.

Tassels can be made by wrapping yarn around a piece of cardboard and tying the top, as shown. Clip at the bottom. Wind another piece of cord tight around the strands a few times about 1/2 inch or 1 inch below the tie and knot to create the tassel shape. Trim ends.

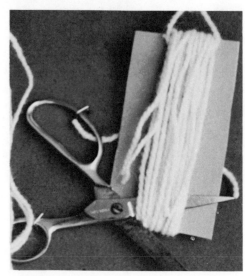

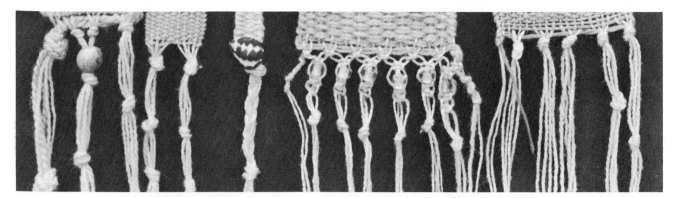

Square knots and different-sized overhand knots with beads strung on can be used for endings. Detail, Lee Erlin Snow.

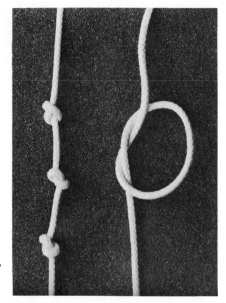

The overhand knot is simple to make, versatile, decorative, and efficient. It holds threads together and prevents ends from unraveling, and it can be made with one or more threads.

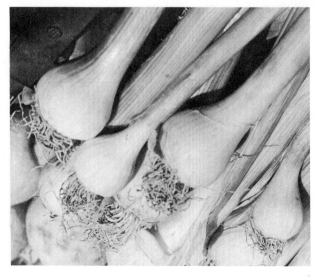

Ideas for endings can be suggested by man-made and natural objects. Above, beads on display in Mexico. Right, scallions could be interpreted in an ending using cords, beads, overhand knots, and teased endings.

SOFT HANGING. Martha Underwood. 45 inches high, 30 inches wide. Weaving, crochet, and mixed techniques. One way to work is to begin with a sketch such as the one below so that you have some idea of the project. Usually the work will differ greatly from the sketch, but that's perfectly all right. Many works grow and develop as they progress.

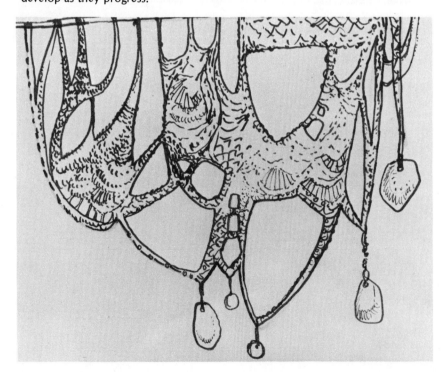

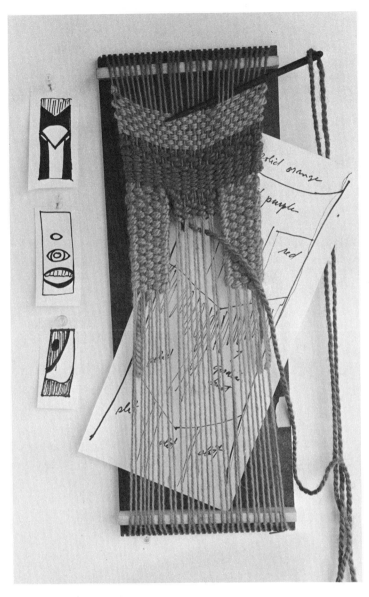

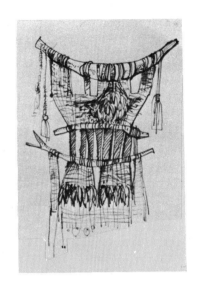

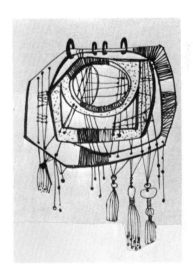

You may wish to sketch a design and place it beneath your weaving as you work so that you can roughly follow the outline for shaping and color fill. A series of small sketches can be developed into valid woven compositions.

These sketches (right), by Martha Underwood, are from a sketch book she keeps handy. She may develop some of these weavings or use parts of one with portions of another.

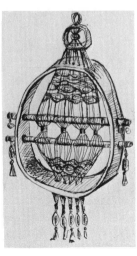

IDEAS FOR WEAVING DESIGNS

Many objects in your environment can suggest ideas for weavings or portions of them. The artist constantly filters what he sees through his artistic eye and interprets his observations into shapes and forms adaptable to his particular craft. The following photos are offered to stimulate design concepts and motifs that can be used in weaving. They are presented, also, in the hope that they will help the reader expand his own visions and to see everyday things in new ways. Additional photos are shown in several other chapters in which they may apply to the design created.

ARCHES IN PORTUGAL might be worked into a complete woven tapestry. It is perfect for sketching and putting beneath your warps. Follow the design with different-colored yarns using dovetailing, interlocking, slit stitching, and others.

The gnarled tree forms with sprigs of branches turned upside down stimulate an excellent idea for endings in a weaving.

Ideas for patterns can be as close as your refrigerator. The repeat pattern on a pineapple can be readily developed into a weaving.

Seaweed at minus tide might suggest areas of loose yarn combined with solid shapes. It could suggest free-form weaves. *Photo, Lois Constantine.*

Sausages hanging in a market can suggest rhythmic designs in a two-dimensional weaving or draping ideas for sculptural form. Joyce Richards often works her woven shapes into forms that are similar to these. (See pages 49, 64.)

A close-up of the mane of a stone lion takes on a new visual aspect and illustrates many directions for wefts to take.

A basket of zucchini might stimulate the placement of shapes in a double weave or of color areas in a crochet.

TREE BURL.

BLUE AND GREEN. Martha
Underwood. 56 inches high, 12
inches wide. Weaving, wrapping,
braiding, and knotting using
horsehair, jute, and other yarns.

BLUE AND GREEN (detail).
Martha Underwood. The rich raised
swirling pattern and underlays in
this detail could be compared to
the burl of a tree, opposite.

4 Frames and Boards

One of the most popular methods for weaving off-loom is to use a portable flat frame or board that holds the warp taut. Use an old picture frame or artist's canvas stretcher bars, which are available in various lengths. Three or four pairs of bars in different sizes offer a versatile system for making weavings up to about 20 inches by 30 inches. Larger weavings are not so portable, and a frame with legs, shown on page 62, may be more efficient than a picture frame. Any size frame can be made from lengths of 1- by-2-inch-wide hardwood. Be sure the corners are solidly assembled and that the rough edges are smoothed so as not to catch the yarn. A convenient portable weaving board that follows the same basic principles of a frame is also illustrated.

The top and bottom bars of the frame can be notched to keep the warp spaced evenly and in place. A spring curtain rod stretched and nailed to the top and bottom edges of the frame also will hold the warp in position. Another practical method is to hammer nails along the top and bottom edges of a decorative frame and wind the warp on the nails. When the weaving is accomplished, it remains in the frame permanently.

Some weavers prefer to separate the warp with *heddles*, which are used to lift each set of warps similarly to but more efficiently than a shed stick (page 23). Weavers tend to devise their own systems; to illustrate each weaver's favorite frame and working method would require a book in itself. This variety emphasizes the freedom involved in weaving techniques and results.

When a weaving larger than the single height of the frame is planned, weave the front surface first; then rotate the warp around the frame. A round dowel rod taped or hammered to the top and bottom of the frame will make rotating the weaving easier. It is possible to weave two or more shapes and assemble them.

BELL TOWER. Joyce Richards. 36 inches high, 20 inches wide. Many kinds of yarns were woven in two flat sections on a frame. Some areas were folded over for the lath-like side strips. Other sections were folded and sewn. The center section at the top was double woven so that two layers would result.

A frame is warped by tying the thread around the top molding, winding the threads evenly around the frame, and tying the last thread off at the bottom. After the first few rows are woven, using front and back threads, the warps may be separated with a shed stick.

Notch a frame at top and bottom to keep the warps spaced evenly. Make notches with a hand drill, a sharp knife, or a coping saw. Distance between the warps determines the density of the weave. If you weave to the top and bottom edges, do not cut the loops or the weaving may unravel. Slip them off and place them on a rod or other hanging device or tie individual threads around each warp and place the threads on the rod. Additional threads may be added to the bottom loops for fringe and other ending treatments.

A frame may also be warped with a figure 8. Pass the thread over the top molding and through the frame center to the back of and around the bottom molding. Reverse on each alternate wind so that the threads are crossed at top and bottom. Precrossing in the figure 8 sometimes makes it easier to pick the separate warps as you weave. To keep the warps in one plane twine across the top row so that all the warp threads from front and back are held in one weaving plane.

Opposite page left: double weaving means weaving the top warps separately from the warps behind the frame. Two layers of fabric result. To make it easier on your eyes, place a piece of cardboard or sheet of paper between the warp layers as you weave. At any point the layers may be joined with the same weft. The same system is used for tubular weaving, in which portions are woven together vertically and the layers are stuffed.

Single, Double, and Tubular Weaves

A *single* weave consists of one layer of fabric and uses all the warps on the frame simultaneously on one plane. For a *double* weave, the warps on the front of the frame are woven separately from the warps at the back, and two layers of fabric result. The layers may be separate, or they may be joined in one or more places by weaving wefts into one or both layers. When double weaving front and back layers separately, two wefts are used, but they may be interchanged when the layers are to be connected. If the double weave is connected on one side only, it can be opened up into one large shape after it is removed from the frame. A *tubular* weave results when the double layers are woven together at the sides and/or in other portions of the work. The two layers then may be stuffed for a three-dimensional form.

Finished weaving. Mieke Solari. Natural yarns, including homespun woolens, alpaca, goathair, camel's hair, and human hair. *Photo, Barbara Painter.*

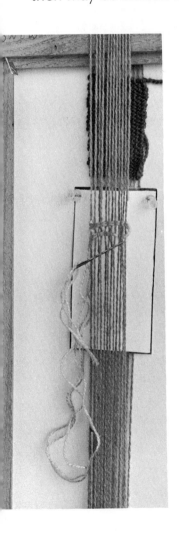

Double weaving in progress by Mieke Solari uses the warp on the top layer of the frame separately from the warp on the bottom layer. The top layer is planned with many negative areas so that the bottom layer shows through.

A weaving remains on the back of a decorative frame on which it is worked. Hammer broad-head nails along the top and bottom of the back inside rim of the frame. Wind the warp around the nails from top to bottom. Select yarns that blend with the finish of the frame.

With a long steel needle the shapes were worked around with tabby from the back of the frame. You can check the appearance and work from both back and front of the frame.

The finished weaving. Lee Erlin Snow. 12 inches high, 15 inches wide.

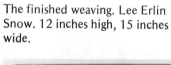

Shapes of suede and leather were woven into the warp.

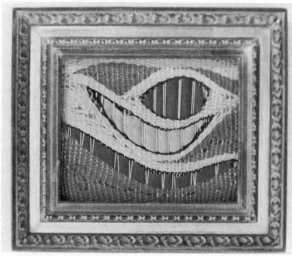

INDIAN MOTIF. Lee Erlin Snow. 24 inches high, 18 inches wide. Copper nails used for holding the warp are placed on the front of the walnut frame and become part of the design. Projecting parts are reinforced with light wire.

GATE OF SUPREME HAPPINESS. Lee Erlin Snow. 36 inches square. Weaving is worked from warp wound on nails in back of frame. It is based on a design suggested by Japanese Shinto gates.

An efficient weaving board can be purchased or made in a variety of sizes and is based on the same principle as a frame. A piece of rigid pressboard such as Masonite is evenly notched at top and bottom. A strip of 1/2-inch pine is glued and nailed about 1/2 inch from the top and bottom. These are not notched. Notches can be made about 1/8 inch apart and warped close together or far apart, depending upon the yarn used and density desired.

Tape the beginning and end threads at the back of the board. The board may be warped with different colors and types of thread.

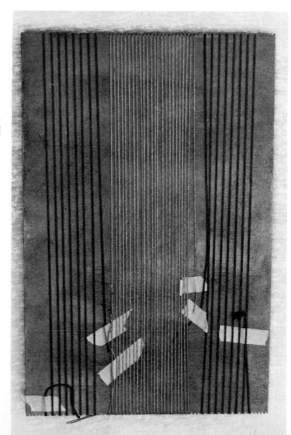

When the weaving is finished, the warp is cut at the back, and the work is removed from the board. The head and ends are then finished. The weft threads can be brought around the back of the work and woven in so that they don't show. They may also be braided and knotted for a more interesting finish.

Wefts can be worked in many patterns up and down the board and then filled in with other threads and patterns. It is not necessary to work in a rigid horizontal progression. Observe that wefts are also brought around the back of the board so that the work will pull even at the sides.

A board that is warped too tight will tend to buckle, and it may crack or break.

Board weaving with inserts of fur (detail). Lee Erlin Snow. Observe the use of different thicknesses and types of yarns and the various weaves used in open and closed areas. Sections of unwoven warp create a vertical motif.

Assorted weavings created on the weaving board have been combined with beads, twigs for headings, bells, shells, nuts, and other objects. The excess warp cut from the center back becomes the fringes used at the bottom and the yarns used for the headings. Lee Erlin Snow.

A pillow in progress on a frame loom made from a beach chair back. Susan Lyttle. Weavings can progress from bottom to top or from top to bottom. The needle, a skewer used for trussing poultry, works well after the tip has been filed down and blunted. *Courtesy, Artist.*

A frame may be tied to any upright post for stability. The warp is threaded into a wood heading, and the heading is tied to the frame. The warp is also wound through holes in the wood heading and around the bottom of the frame. If the tension loosens, the strings that hold the heading can be tightened. If more slack is needed, the strings can be loosened. *Photo, Lee Erlin Snow.*

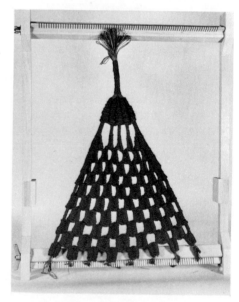

A frame with adjustable top- and bottom-notched rods, called a Todd loom, is usually associated with simple shapes for beginning weavers. Stana Coleman improvises the frame for a triangular weaving that includes wrapping around alternating sets of warps. The finished piece was removed from the frame and attached to holding rods.

SANTA CLAUS AND SAILOR
BOY DOLLS. Momo Nagano.
About 14 inches high. Rya and
tapestry weaves.

Momo Nagano nails together four
pieces of old scrap wood and
attaches pieces from broom handles
at top and bottom so that she can
rotate the weaving. The broom
handles are notched to hold the
warp, which has been wound on in
a tubular warp (see page 51) and
held together at the top with
chaining. The doll was woven front
and back as one piece; then it was
cut off the frame. The sides were
woven together with a needle, and
the piece was stuffed.

OSTRICH GIRL WITH LION
MAN. Momo Nagano. 20 inches
high, 35 inches wide. Weaving on a
simple frame. Portions are double
woven. Weaves include tabby, leno
(near top and in several other
areas), which exposes weave
beneath, ghiordes knot, and others.
The fringe is made from top warp
threads. The girl's skirt can be lifted.

Detail of Momo Nagano's piece
(left) shows the weave beneath the
dress. At top left, the crossover of
the leno weave.

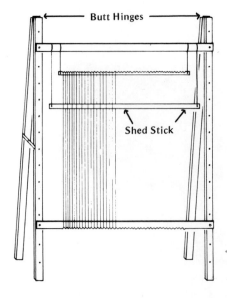

Butt Hinges

Shed Stick

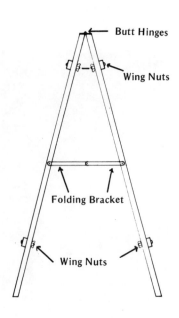

Butt Hinges

Wing Nuts

Folding Bracket

Wing Nuts

Frances Weber works large weavings on a frame that is supported in the same way as an artist's easel. Small frames are too flimsy for the tension needed in a wide and long warp. Actually, two frames are hinged back to back for support. The frame may be collapsed and stored. It could be used by two people at the same time and adapted for a classroom as well as a studio. For two frames you will need four boards approximately 4 feet long by 2 inches wide by 1/3 inch thick for the uprights. For the horizontal boards use four pieces about 30 inches long, 2 inches wide, and 3/4 inch thick. Holes are drilled at each end of the horizontal boards and along the side of the uprights. The horizontals may be notched. They are held to the uprights by wing nuts so that they are adjustable for different-sized weavings. The size of the frame can be altered because the uprights and horizontals can be made to any desired dimension.

The frame may be warped directly around the two horizontals as with any other frame, or it may be warped using a rod, as shown. This rod is securely fastened to the top horizontal by strings and may be tightened if the warps loosen. The rod becomes the heading of the piece.

Weave a yardstick or other suitable stick through the warps to act as a shed. Drill holes in each end of the shed to suspend it to the top horizontal so that it will not fall away. Weaving can proceed from top down or from bottom up.

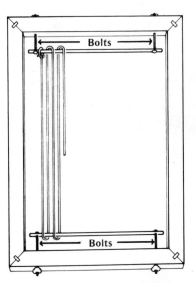

Bolts

Bolts

A frame can also be fitted with bolts that hold the tension bars. These can be loosened and tightened as necessary to adjust the tautness of the warp.

A ready-to-use frame, made by Lily, combines the convenience of the board and frame. Included with the Lilette are a wooden and wire shuttle and shed sticks. Here it is shown warped and ready for weaving. A strip of masking tape placed over the warp notches will prevent the warp from pulling out.

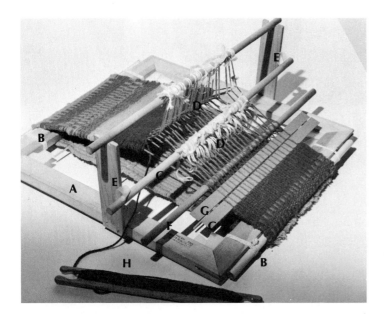

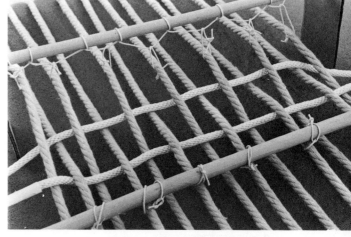

This portable frame may appear more complicated than it is. The parts include:

A) Four canvas stretcher bars for the frame.

B) Dowels tied on at top and bottom to rotate weaving.

C) Two dowels that serve as heddle bars.

D) Heddles, strings passed around the warps and tied to the heddle bars. One set of heddles lifts the even-numbered warps; when raised, it lifts that set of warps to create the shed. The second set of heddles raises and lowers the odd-numbered warps.

E) A piece of wood with a groove at top center. The wood is nailed to each side of the frame to hold the heddle bar when it is raised.

F) Warp end bar. Bar is warped in as shown in the drawing below.

G) Tension sticks. Two or more flat pieces of cardboard can be woven into the warps to take up any slack. As the weaving progresses and the warp tightens up, the tension sticks are removed.

H) Shuttle. The shuttle holds the wound weft and is passed through the shed held open by the heddles.

Heddle bars are easily fashioned from two dowel rods of the same width as the frame. Shown are two simple ways to tie heddles so that the warps can slide through. Top bar has a chain of half hitches. An individual heddle string is passed around each warp and tied to each loop between the half hitches. Lifting the heddle then raises alternate warps to create the shed.

The bottom bar shows each heddle string passed around the warp, wound twice around the bar, and secured with a square knot. Fine wire or string can be used for heddles.

To warp a frame with a warp end bar, follow the diagram. Before you begin, tape or tie the warp end bar to back of frame to prevent it from slipping. Mark the bar with pencil lines to indicate where you want warp to begin and end and mark the spacing for the warps. Begin with a knot on the warp end bar and wind yarn tight. The warp should be taut when you finish. You can also add tension sticks by taping them as you warp. End the warping by tying a knot at the other side of the bar and remove tape holding the warp end bar and tension sticks.

The horizontal members of the frame could also be made from two lengths of round pipe set into two wood vertical bars; these simplify the rotation of the weaving.

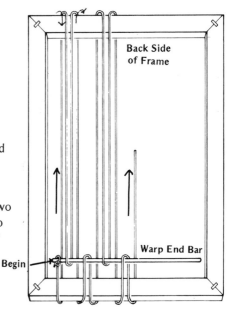

Back Side of Frame

Warp End Bar

Begin

SAFARI. Joyce Richards. 36 inches high, 23 inches wide. Tubular and flat areas are made on a frame. The doughnut shapes are papier mâché wrapped with yarn. Wool, orlon, and mohair yarns are used; corks and bells are added.

SILHOUETTES AND SHADOWS. Joyce Richards. 30 inches high, 20 inches wide. The black and white weaving was woven flat on a frame, and portions were folded in some areas for a relief dimension. The white is unspun alpaca with black seed beads.

ROOM DIVIDER (in progress).
Libby Platus. Room-sized weavings
are often woven without looms or
frames. The weaver must devise the
necessary apparatus. Libby Platus
strung chains from hooks on the
beams of her living room ceiling for
a large sculpture commission that
includes weaving, knotting, and
wrapping hundreds of yards of
ropes. Many of the sculptural
weavings illustrated in Chapter 7
were developed in a similar manner.

5 Cardboard and Other Devices

Weavings can be many shapes. In the previous chapter, we showed how to weave on frames. Many other devices also can be employed for creating any variety of shapes, such as circles, triangles, abstract, three-dimensional and free-forms, and so forth. The ideas for weaving on a cardboard can be expanded depending upon the shape you have in mind. The principle behind weaving on a cardboard involves cutting a pattern and then filling in the shape of the pattern with weaving. A cardboard shape can be two or three dimensional to yield any type of geometric solid that can be supported by a wire, piece of plastic, or other type of armature woven into the shape.

When you plan a design, it is wise to cut the shape in paper first and then outline it on cardboard. Notch the edges of the cardboard for warping. Sturdy cardboard that won't bend, such as the platters used for delicatessen trays, corrugated cardboard from boxes, or heavy Bristol board, is ideal.

Cardboard can be adapted to shapes for collars, cuffs, hangings, pockets on a dress, an addition to a throw pillow, a piece of furniture, jacket, or other accessory. Entire front and back panels of clothing can be woven on a one-piece cardboard pattern, as shown in the examples by Momo Nagano and Earlene Ahrens.

When shapes are wider at one edge than the other, more warping notches are needed at the larger edge, or it may be necessary to carry the warp around one notch twice. Warping can be accomplished by passing the threads around the back of the board or by winding them around the notch and back down the front. Where patterns widen and additional warps are necessary, place a T pin in the cardboard, add a warp around the pin, and wind it to the bottom of the board. Then weave the additional warp into the pattern in the next row.

Cardboard platters used for pizzas and delicatessen trays are perfect for circles, collars, and other odd shapes. A knitting rake (bottom left) can also be warped in one or two directions for weaving, combined with stitchery, knotting, and other techniques. The only other materials you need are yarn, needles, a pair of scissors, and a beater.

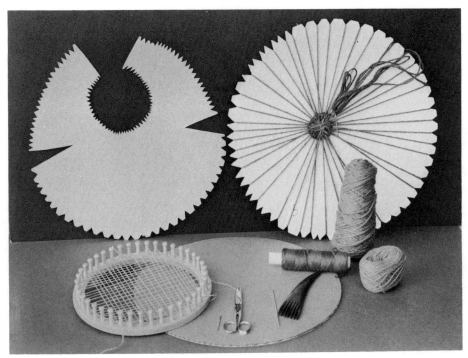

Cardboard cut in the shape of a vest front is warped horizontally. The warps are held at the neckline with pins. Observe how the major shapes and color areas are woven in first. Tabby or plain weave will be used for filling in.

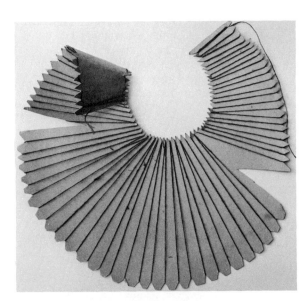

Warp can be carried all around the back, as is shown on the first row. However, you can warp around the points of the notches only for a closely finished edge. If you warp around the notches rather than all around the back, there will be fewer ends to tuck in. Observe that the inner collar notches may have to be warped twice to compensate for the wider arc at the bottom.

A round notched cardboard is warped by carrying the threads across the diameter, around the notches, and back again until it is warped as densely as desired.

Tie the threads together at the center of the circle but pass the thread under so that you gather all of them under the tie thread. You can use the same color thread as the warp; a contrasting color has been used here for demonstration.

Before you begin, tie the end of the weft thread to a warp to prevent the thread from slipping out as you work.

Threading several folds through the needle helps to shorten the thread as you work and allows you to pull out length as needed. Here only one thread is used at a time for the actual weaving, but you can use two or more weft threads simultaneously.

Ends can be finished by tucking them under and weaving them in, but don't cut the ends short until you are sure you have used all you want for threading on beads, bells, buttons, or whatever. If necklines, waistbands, cuffs, and other edges are too large or too stretchy, finish them with one or two rows of crochet to pull them together and to keep the desired shape.

When weaving in objects, such as feathers, raffia, and other hard-to-anchor items, it's a good idea to dab on some fabric glue for extra security.

For cardboard weaving, use any and all of the weaves already illustrated in Chapter 3.

Weaving progresses over and under. When you weave a circular shape, you may have to pass the weft under and over two or more warps at the inner part of the circle so that it will lie as flat as the wider arc of the circle. You may also sketch a shape or pattern directly onto the circle so that you can follow it as you weave.

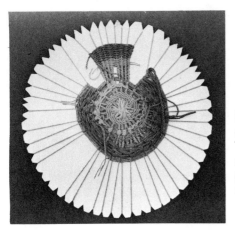

Many different shapes can be developed within a circular form. The small part of this form may be attached to a neck band, and the piece may be used as a front panel on a dress or as a piece of jewelry.

The weaving, cut off the cardboard, has many loose ends, which can be used for beads, for knotting, or for a braided or tasseled fringe. Ends may be woven back under the shape and clipped short. If the piece is to be worn as jewelry, a lining is a nice finishing touch. The piece may also be sewn to a dress, a furniture cushion, or a throw pillow. Lee Erlin Snow.

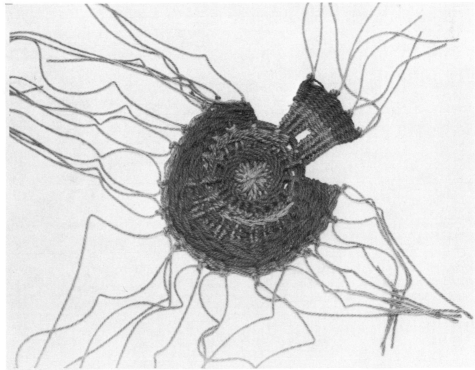

INCA COLLAR. Lee Erlin Snow.
Woven on an irregular shaped
cardboard with a variety of dull and
shiny yarns, leather, and feathers.

COLLAR. Annabel Bergstrom.
Woven on cardboard using rug and
chenille yarn, velvet strips, unspun
wool, beads, and feathers.

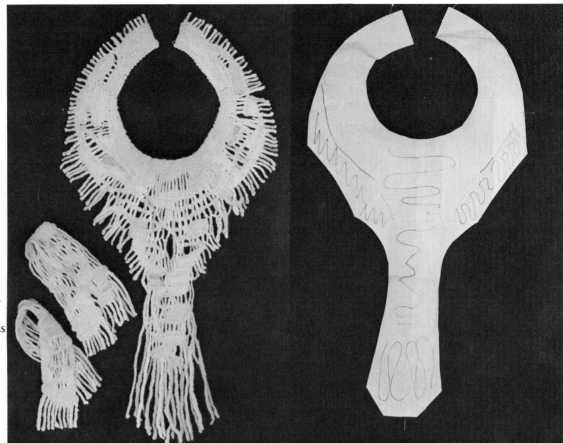

Matching collar and cuffs. Helen Hennessey. Lace and tabby weaves worked in a variety of shapes and novelty yarns. First the pattern was cut from brown paper; then it was traced onto a cardboard cut to the same shape, notched, and used for weaving.

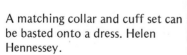

A matching collar and cuff set can be basted onto a dress. Helen Hennessey.

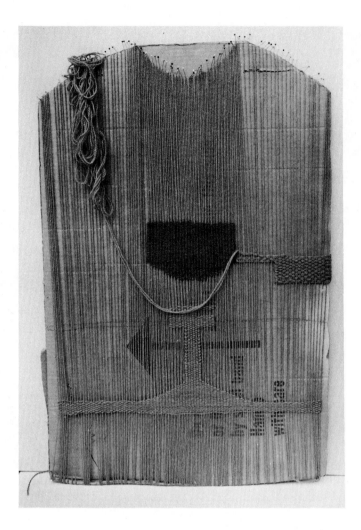

A large cardboard panel from a corrugated cardboard box has been shaped similarly to the finished poncho on the page opposite. The designs beneath the weaving were on the box and are not the sketch for the pattern; however, you may sketch your design on the board.

Pins hold the warp along the top edge and shape the neckline.

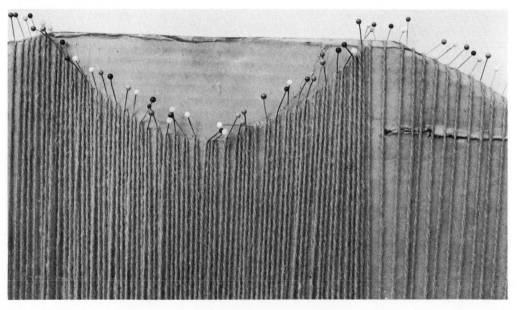

PONCHO (front). Momo Nagano.
Woven on a cardboard shape.

PONCHO (rear). Momo Nagano.

There are many ways to create a woven purse. It can be made in two panels and joined at the side. Another method is to double weave, using the front and back of the warp separately and weaving the sides together in a tubular effect. By Phyllis Hall. *Photo, Clement Hall.*

Purse panel patterns can be cut to any shape. Handles may be made separately and the pieces assembled as shown. When an extra lip is needed to be wound around a wood handle, allow for fold-over when you cut the cardboard pattern.

Purses woven on boards and
cardboards. Top, Melicent Saylor;
left, Betty Dickerhoff; right,
Earlene Ahrens.

PULLOVER. Earlene Ahrens.
Sleeve shapes were included in the
cardboard pattern. The garment
was woven as two pieces; then the
front and back were assembled.

SEA ANEMONE. Eileen Bernard.
Triangular shaped piece with jute
warp gathered with an overhand
knot, strung through a large
wooden bead, and knotted again.
Ends are wrapped.

WEAVING ON A PILLOW. Lee Erlin Snow. A free-form shape woven on cardboard is sewn to the face of a hand-woven pillow. *Photo, Lee Erlin Snow.*

THE SUN. Sharon LaPierre. 29 inches wide, 29 inches across. A circular shape woven on a frame is extended to an odd shape by the addition of a stuffed and stitched felt border. *Courtesy, Artist.*

WOVEN PALM FROND. Sally Turpie. The branches of the palm frond were used as warp for the bands of colored weaving and wrapping. *Photographed at the Yarn Depot, San Francisco.*

6 Hoops and Other Objects

Weavers' preoccupation with shape, in addition to the materials of the craft, has led them to experiment with many objects for weaving. Often these objects remain an integral part of the weaving after it has been completed. Objects employed in a weaving can be twigs, rings, wood and wire wheels, junk, and armatures especially created for the purpose. Weavers have discovered that anything that can be warped can serve as a loom, or basis, for weaving. Regardless of what is warped, the weaving procedures are the same. Often more innovation and creativity are required to make an unusual form work as a weaving.

Circular forms of any size can be developed using the principles illustrated in the drawings suggested by Frances Weber. The same principles can be devised for oblong shapes, free-forms, and combinations of one shape within another, each warped individually and then assembled. All the techniques shown can be adapted for single or double weaving, for hangings, and for utilitarian items.

When an object is to remain within the weaving as an armature, it may be made from any material that has the desired shape. The object is then warped and woven into. Often the shapes are made from mundane items, such as bent clothes hangers, branches, and found objects. As such, the object may be wrapped or knotted around. It may be completely covered so it is no longer important for its own shape but only for the shape it gives to the weaving.

Examples throughout this chapter should be studied for the forms, the weaves, and the endings used.

Woven shapes by Momo Nagano illustrate the validity of moving a weaving off a traditional loom and onto found objects for beautiful statements with fibers and shapes. Bottom, an embroidery hoop is wrapped and parts are warped and woven in a double (two-layer) weave. Center, a modern interpretation of an Indian loom made from twigs becomes an integral part of the finished work. Top, a rusted, discarded strainer rim and handle found new life as the basis for a weaving.

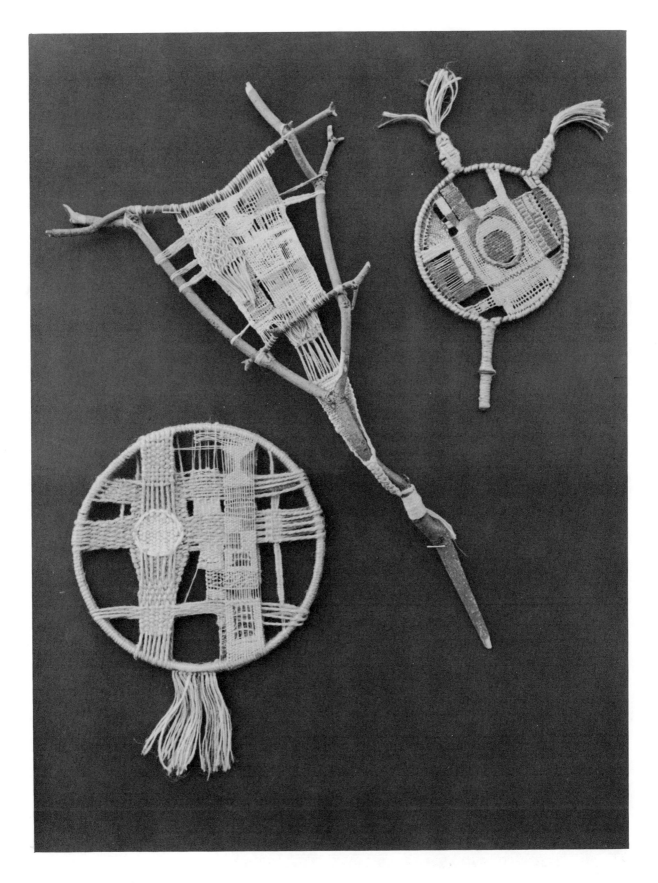

A circular shape can be developed many ways from different materials to yield different effects within the circle. This 15-inch-diameter circle, cut from 1/8-inch Masonite, is more durable than cardboard. It has an uneven number of 1/4-inch notches along the edge, spaced approximately 1/3 inch apart.

The circle is warped by passing the yarn from one notch across to the other and either across the back clockwise or around the notches in order until all the notches are filled. Tie the yarn in the center, as shown on page 68, and begin to weave. By placing your hand under approximately half the threads you can actually separate fan-shaped groups of warps top and bottom to make it easier to weave with a large

steel needle. Weave outward by dividing the two lower fan shapes into four groups. Weave over, under, and around this lower group until you are about 1/2 to 1 inch out from the center. Repeat on the top group until the two layers can be joined without too much bunching in the center. If you weave along the outer edge and beat the yarn to the center as you develop the pattern, you won't be so likely to miss warp threads. All the weaving patterns shown in Chapter 3 can be employed. You can weave sections and work either from the center out or from the edge to the center.

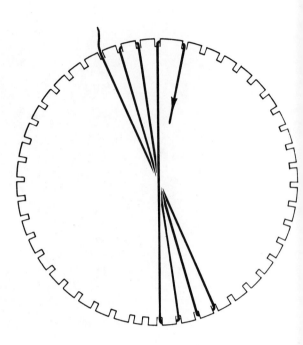

THE TIMID LION. Frances Weber. 15 inches in diameter. Made on the solid loom above. White wool yarn in tabby and twill weaves were used to shape the face; rya knots form the mane. The hanging was stuffed from the back for shape and dimension. *Collection, Mr. and Mrs. James R. Franklin, Tennessee.*

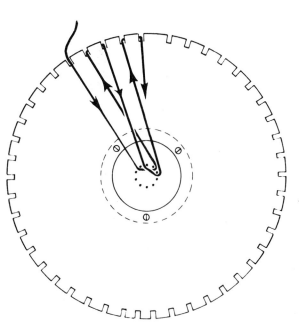

OPEN-CENTER CIRCLE

Making a circle with a center hole eliminates the hump of gathered center threads that results in the solid circle. This circle is 15-inch-diameter (any diameter can be used) 1/8-inch Masonite and is notched. A 4-inch-diameter circle was cut out of the center. Another circle, of 3/4-inch plywood and 5 inches in diameter, was cut to fit under the center hole of the large round. Three matching holes were drilled in both circles so that the 5-inch wood circle fits beneath the hole in the masonite and can be removed with bolts and nuts. Ten small holes were drilled in the 5-inch under circle, and finishing nails were inserted.

To warp, begin at an outer notch and pass the threads to the nails in the center, back out to the next notch, and so on all around (do not go around the back). There are more outer edge notches than center nails, so each nail will carry approximately ten threads.

When the weaving is complete, thread a very strong piece of string or yarn through the loops on the center nails. Unbolt the plywood disc and remove it from the back. Draw the string together very tight, tie for a neat center, and weave.

GOLD PILLOW. Frances Weber. Approximately 15 inches in diameter. Woven on the open center circle, it permits a neat open middle hole; it can be closed when the loops are pulled together tight. *Courtesy, Artist.*

LICHEN. Frances Weber. 15 inches in diameter. This hanging also is woven on the open center circle. A lampshade ring was placed at the edge and woven in to provide rigidity. *Collection, Maria Pitner, Tennessee.*

WEAVING ON RINGS

Rings are very popular for weaving. Some people warp them, but they struggle to keep the warp threads evenly spaced. One way to work efficiently is to anchor rings of metal, plastic, wire, or other material to a piece of Celotex or cork board with nails also used to warp. Space nails evenly around the ring into the Celotex about 1/2 inch apart. Additional rings or odd-shaped objects can also be anchored into the board in any position you like—centered, off-centered, or whatever.

Begin warping at the outside directly from the cone or ball of yarn and carry the yarn on top of the outer ring and over the center ring. Return under the center ring, under the outer ring, around two nails, over the top of the outer rings, over the center ring, and back again. Continue around the ring until complete. The nails serve the same purpose as the spacers or notches in other setups. It will be necessary to readjust tension as you warp because of the off-centering.

Ideas for shapes and designs in a round and off-center round form can be suggested by scenes around you, such as this old wheel with chains.

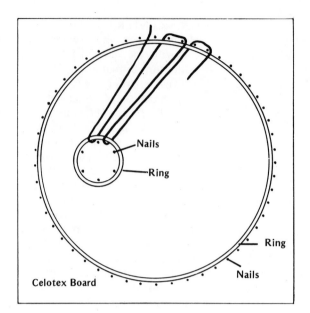

SAND DOLLARS. Frances F. Jones. 60 inches high, 30 inches wide. Clayware rings were designed with holes in them especially for warping, and they were anchored on the Celotex board. When all the rings were complete, they were joined with several strands of yarn, which were wrapped. The whole group of rings was attached to an iron frame by needle-weaving. *Collection, Mr. & Mrs. Douglas Nelson, Tennessee. Courtesy, Artist.*

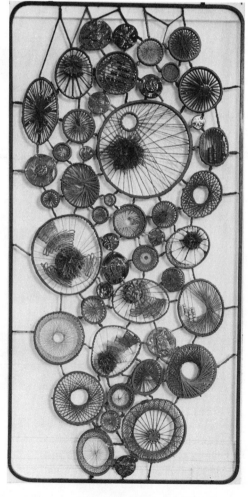

WEAVING ON A CYLINDER

A cylindrical weaving can be made on any size tube. This one is fashioned from a 13-inch-diameter, 40-inch-long paper tube (such tubes are often discarded by manufacturers of folding cartons). A piece of plywood is cut to fit inside the tube top and recessed down to allow for a thickness of a piece of Celotex of the same diameter. Nails through the cardboard will hold the plywood in place. This kind of tube can be warped in any way desired. It was used to create CAROUSEL, at right.

A piece of Styrofoam was rounded and covered with paper to fit on top of the core and provide a sloped weaving surface. Lampshade rings were held at top and bottom with nails (also used for warping) placed over and under to prevent slipping. Another row of nails near the bottom is used to tie the warps down. Lengths of warps were looped from top center to top ring and then to bottom ring. Groups of these warps were tied to the tension nails.

After the top portion was woven, additional warps were strung between the two rings to achieve a denser weave and an interesting pattern. When the piece was finished, the nails holding the rings in place were removed, the cylindrical weaving was lifted off the core, and the bottom was finished.

By varying the size of the rings and cores used, you can make any number of different forms. Weaving can progress from the bottom ring up or from the top down.

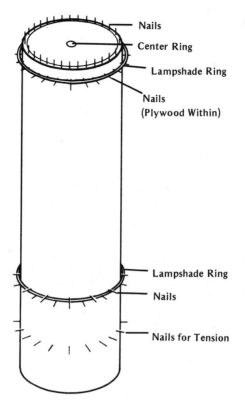

Nails
Center Ring
Lampshade Ring
Nails (Plywood Within)
Lampshade Ring
Nails
Nails for Tension

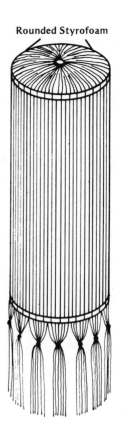

Rounded Styrofoam

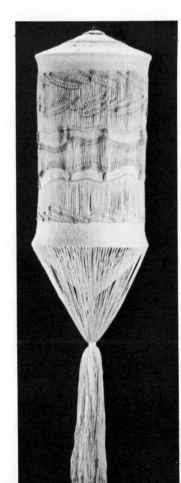

CAROUSEL. Frances C. Weber. 65 inches high, 17 inches in diameter. The finished weaving made on the cylinder. Plain and twill weaves were used on the top. Spanish lace and plain weave were used on the tubular section.

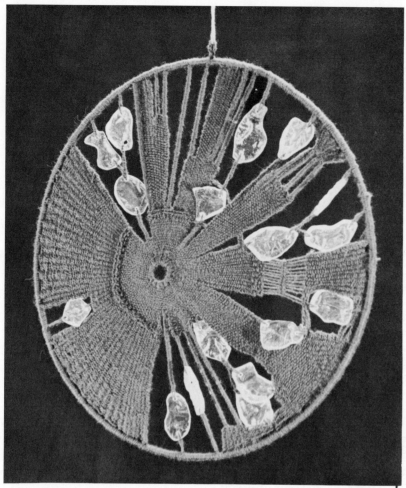

REFLECTIONS. Frances C. Weber. 19 inches in diameter. Worked with rings held in place onto a Celotex board. *Courtesy, Artist.*

HOOP DOUBLE WEAVE (detail) Momo Nagano. This piece illustrates the two layers and the variety of weaves incorporated.

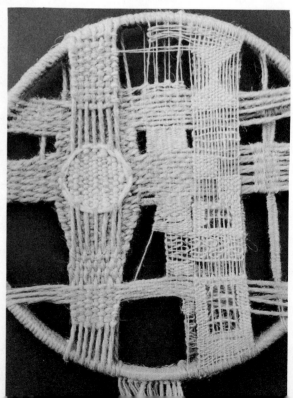

CIRCULAR TAPESTRY. Barbara
Wittenberg. Approximately 25
inches in diameter. Weft twining
was used for most of the flat areas.
Also used are rya and ghiordes
knots and feathers.

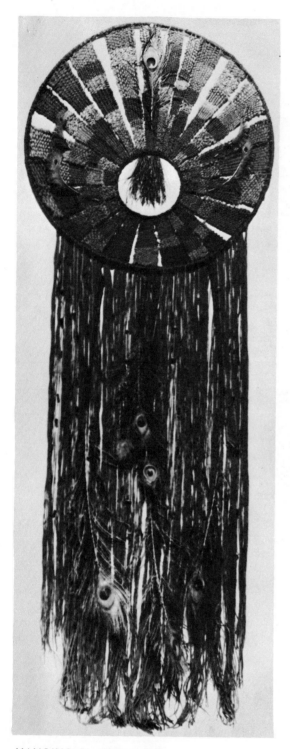

HANGING (detail). Phyllis Hall.
Photo, Clement Hall.

HANGING. Phyllis Hall. 7 feet
high, 36 inches in diameter. Two
hoops woven in an off-center
arrangement using the slit, tabby,
and twining techniques and
incorporating peacock feathers.
Photo, Clement Hall.

BROKEN CIRCLE. Tina Krythe.
24 inches high, 16 inches in
diameter. Weaving with knotted
sections on half of a wire hoop.

HANGING. Linda Borlund. A hoop
can be slightly bent for an oval
shape and warped with or without
center rings. This piece illustrates a
great variety of shapes and weaving
details. *Photo, Lee Erlin Snow, at
the Egg and the Eye Gallery, Los
Angeles.*

CIRCULAR FORM (detail).
Marianne Rodwell. 36 inches in
diameter. Natural bamboo strips
form the warp, which is then woven
and strung with wooden beads.

MANDALA. Stana Coleman. 24
inches in diameter. Weaving was
worked on a knitting rake. When it
was removed, the outer loops were
slipped off the pegs, and the piece
was mounted onto a felt-covered
circle of plywood.

GALACTIC HYDRA. Pat Swenson.
6 feet high, 3 feet in diameter.
Ceiling-suspended free form was
woven on steel hoops placed
parallel to the floor. *Courtesy, Artist.*

EQUESTRIAN. Pat Swenson. 36
inches in diameter. Weaving of
black and rust-colored yarns on a
rusty iron ring. *Courtesy, Artist.*

UNTITLED (detail). Deborah Frederick.

UNTITLED. Deborah Frederick. 31 inches high, 5-1/2 inches wide. A metal coat hanger was bent, warped, and woven with handspun Kentucky cow hair. *Courtesy, Artist.*

ABAKAN RED. Magdalena
Abakanowicz. Sculptural weaving,
on exhibit at the "Deliberate
Entanglements" show, Los Angeles,
1971. *Photo, Richard Gross.*

UNTITLED. Anita Houston. Varied
wools and weaves woven on a frame
loom. *Courtesy, Artist.*

COILED BASKET. Ferne Jacobs.
7 inches high. Waxed linen, metallic
wool, synthetics. *Courtesy, Artist.*

TREE FORM. Ted Hallman.
Knotless netting on wire hoops.
Courtesy, Artist.

COPTIC. Pat Obye. 14 inches high,
10 inches wide. Various weaves and
knots woven on a board.

PORTRAIT. Mary L. Jones. Needle
weaving on a frame. *Courtesy, Artist.*

HANGING (detail). Sylvia Heyden.
Crochet with yak hair. *Courtesy,
Artist.*

GATE OF SUPREME HAPPINESS.
Lee Erlin Snow. Needle weaving on
a frame.

SAFARI. Joyce Richards. 35 inches high, 20 inches wide. Stuffed tubular weaving with assorted yarns and unspun wool.

BRIGHT SHEAF. Susan Brown. Mainly wrapping. *Courtesy, Artist.*

BINGO BASKET. Momo Nagano. 2 feet high, 1 foot wide, 10 inches deep. Warps and weaves using a welded sculpture armature by Max E. Neufeldt. *Photo, Beth Hazard.*

SUNBURST (top view). Liz
Bernstein. 22 inches in diameter.
Woven on a dishwasher frame and
mounted on a board. *Courtesy,
Artist.*

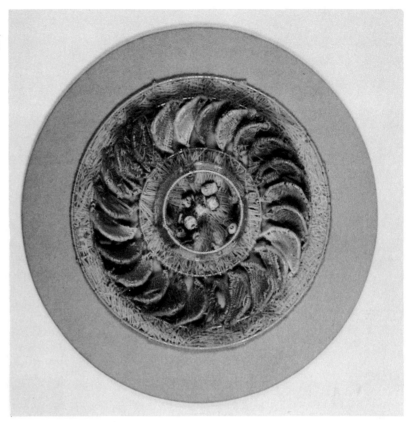

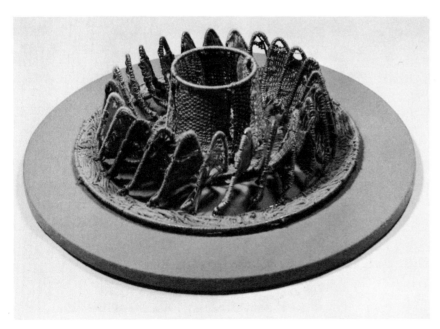

SUNBURST (side view). Liz
Bernstein. *Courtesy, Artist.*

WEAVING ON A RUG BEATER.
Eileen Bernard. 25 inches high, 12
inches wide. Clever adaptation of a
found object shows how
imagination can bring life to a
seemingly useless item.

SPRING HARROW. Shirley Fink.
9-1/2 feet high, 3-1/2 feet wide, 2
feet deep. A rusty spring harrow
was double warped in two
directions with sisal, and the prongs
were allowed to protude. Rya knots
densely covered the warp, and the
ends were unraveled. *Courtesy,
Artist.*

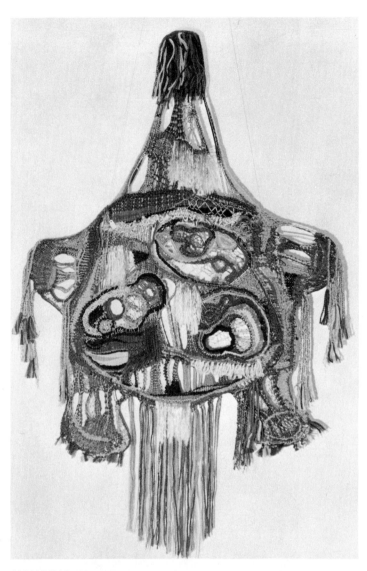

BRIDE OF THE
CYCLOPS. Dorothy Riley. Richly
detailed use of knotting, weaving,
stitchery, and old fishnet with
bone, mirror, jagged teeth, yak tail
hair, and jute. The piece is worked
through spoke holes of an old wood
wheel. *Courtesy, Artist.*

HANGING. Linda Borlund.
Multiple free-form small wire
shapes were combined into one
large shape in this work of brilliant
purples, reds, and pinks. *Photo, Lee
Erlin Snow, at the Egg and the Eye
Gallery, Los Angeles.*

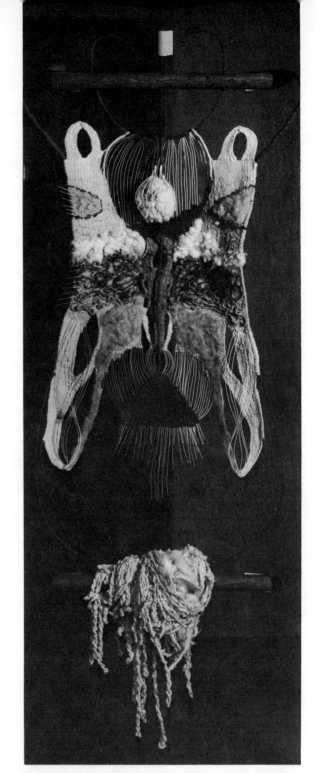

THE LAST BUTTERFLY — A
MUSEUM SPECIMEN. Marianne
Childress. 90 inches high, 36 inches
wide. *Photo, Ron Garrison.*

HANGING WITH MIRROR. Jane
Chapman. *Courtesy, Artist.*

UNTITLED. Joyce Saks. 23 inches high, 21 inches wide. *Photo, David Auerbach.*

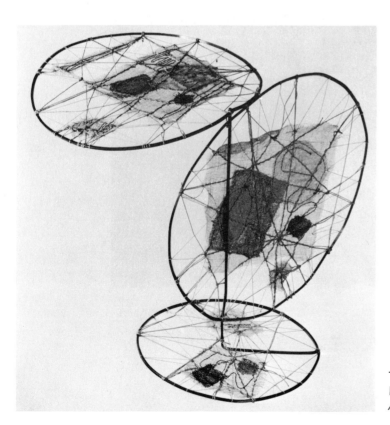

THREE CIRCLES. Winifred Roth. Metal work by Leo Roth. *Courtesy, Artist.*

BALLINGER BRANCH. Momo
Nagano. 24 inches high, 20 inches
wide. Linen weaving on bottle
brush branch. Berries and leaves
were woven in because they fell off
during the weaving process.
*Background oil painting SMILE
by Lee Erlin Snow.*

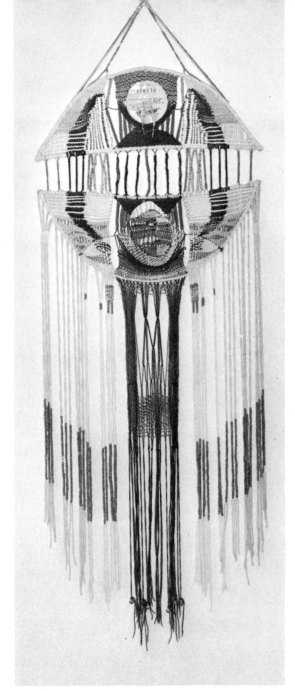

JANUS. Elfleda Russell. 6 feet
high, 2-1/2 feet wide. Weaving,
wrapping, macramé, pulled thread
needle-weaving on shaped wire coat
hanger. *Courtesy, Artist.*

JOKER'S WILD. Elfleda Russell. 5
feet high, 2-1/2 feet wide. Weighted
threads were hung from a rod, and
the weaving moved freely in any
direction alternating between
weaving and macramé. New threads
could be added at any point.
Courtesy, Artist.

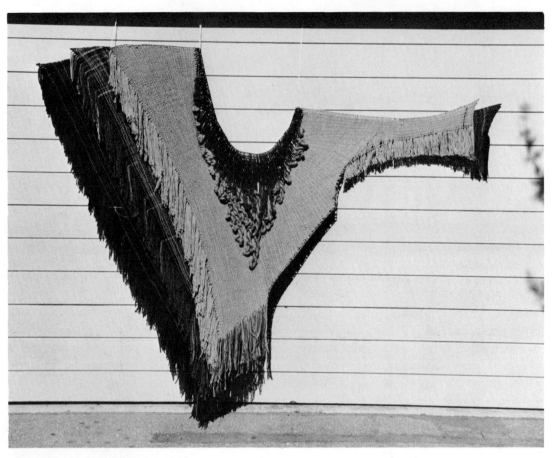

STEEL AND WOOL WEAVING.
Carolyn Potter. 7 feet high, 6 feet
wide, 14 inches deep. Weaving on
three levels of a welded steel frame.
The frame was vertically warped,
and the wefts were inserted by
hand with a crochet hook.
Courtesy, Artist.

ORIENTAL WIG. Lee Erlin Snow.
Wrapping, weaving, and knotting
over a Styrofoam wig stand. Orange
and red jute.

NECKLACE. Virginia H. Barber. Forged copper serves as a loom for the fine copper wire used as warp through small holes drilled in the frame. Wefts are rayon nubby yarn in gold, purple, and turquoise. Bottom rows are long ghiordes knots into which feathers have been wrapped. *Courtesy, Artist.*

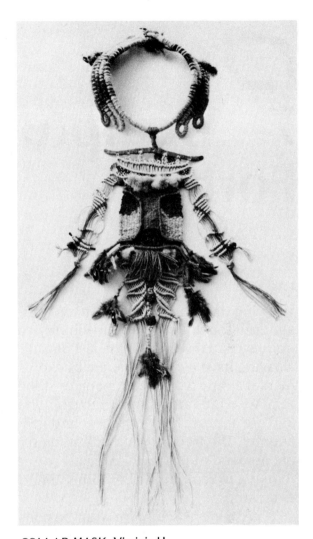

COLLAR MASK. Virginia H. Barber. Collar woven of jute using basket-coiling technique. Bottom suspended from a forged copper bar with holes and warp added for macramé and weaving. Yarn, fur, guinea hen feathers, and ceramic beads. *Courtesy, Artist.*

7 Sculptural Fiber Forms

Weaving traditionally has been associated with fabrics that are used for clothing and furnishings, such as draperies and upholstery. However, in the last decade new statements with weaving have evolved that are as expressive, artistic, and monumental as any work of art made of stone, wood, or metal. Sculptural weavings are winning recognition by serious art collectors and are appearing in museums and galleries throughout the country. The trend toward collecting sculptural weavings has encouraged more avant-garde art communities to open their thinking to sculptural fiber forms and to reexamine weaving as an art.

Weaving as sculpture must be considered an "additive" process. That is, the woven fibers, built up and added to by weaving, must utilize space in the same way a sculptor builds up a clay form. This method for building a fiber sculpture is different from the subtractive sculpture process, in which materials, such as stone or wood, are chipped away. The principles and elements of art must be used in creating with fibers, just as with other media. The weaving must be planned so it has form, shape, line, texture, rhythm, balance, unity, harmony, values, and color relationships and so all these principles and elements work together to achieve a statement that is expressive and pleasing.

The woven sculptures illustrated have been visualized and created in many different ways. The large floor-to-ceiling pieces are often created by stringing the warp from holding beams, then hand weaving the threads, using any method that suits the project and can be devised by the weaver. Often warps are weighted at the bottom if usual methods for holding the warp taut are not feasible. As a particularly large piece progresses, it can become very heavy and may require support afforded by using pulleys

NESKOWIN. Walter Nottingham. 9 feet high, 4 feet wide. Mixed techniques of crocheted and woven horsehair and camel's hair. *Courtesy, "Deliberate Entanglements," UCLA.*

or similar contraptions. Each woven sculpture presents its own engineering problems for creating, assembling, and displaying it, and arriving at a solution to these problems is often as much of a challenge as the actual weaving.

Many of the sculptures illustrated are from the show "Deliberate Entanglements," sponsored by UCLA in 1971. Another show, titled "Sculpture in Fibers" and sponsored by the Museum of Contemporary Crafts, New York, focused on the "one special aspect of this internationally vital movement: forms created entirely without a loom by artists living in America." The trend to sculptural fiber forms has indeed permeated the consciousness of the art world.

AMERICAN PRIMITIVE. Shirley Fink. 5 feet 4 inches high, 5 feet wide. Sisal and jute on rusted holding bars. *Photo, Jim Clayman.*

THREE HANGING SCULPTURES.
Emiko Tokushige. Japan. Left:
white cotton rope. 7-1/2 feet high.
Middle: white cotton rope. 6 feet
high. Right: white cotton rope. 5
feet high. *Courtesy, Artist.*

GRYPHON'S BRINDLED
ROSE. Jean Singerman. 39 inches
high, 19 inches wide, 4 inches deep.
Twined ikat using jute and raffia.
Courtesy, Artist.

CATHEDRAL. Joyce Richards. 60
inches high, 18 inches wide.
Tubular and plain weave stuffed
with dacron. Parts woven on a
frame. Icelandic wool and goathair.
Shards of antique glass are set into
negative areas of weaving to give
a stained-glass effect.

SHAMAN'S SHIELD. Barbara
Waszak Chapman. Approximately 7
feet high. Variety of wools with fur
and beads. Mounted on carved
wood from a piece of old furniture.
*Photo, taken at the Laguna
Museum of Art, Lee Erlin Snow.*

THE CROWD WITHIN. Marianne
Childress. 90 inches high, 24 inches
wide. A detached wood hoop on
the floor carries out the cylindrical
form of the composition. *Photo,
Ron Garrison.*

ABAKAN. Magdalena
Abakanowicz. Poland. Hand-dyed
sisal. *Courtesy, Pasadena Art
Museum.*

POLYPTYQUE. Jagoda Buic.
Yugoslavia. 8 feet high, 17 feet
wide. *Courtesy, "Deliberate
Entanglements," UCLA.*

RED FOREST II. Claire Zeisler. "Slinky" toys are used as armatures and wrapped with fibers for the wiggly forms. *Courtesy, "Deliberate Entanglements," UCLA. Photo, Richard Gross.*

STUDY IN RED. Dorothy Riley. 72 inches high, 18 inches wide, 17 inches deep. Dyed sisal, jute, and string and unspun sisal. *Courtesy, Artist.*

TRAPEZE DE CRISTOBAL. Sheila
Hicks. France. 10 feet high, 4 feet
wide. Free warp and wrapping.
*Courtesy, "Deliberate
Entanglements," UCLA. Photo,
Richard Gross.*

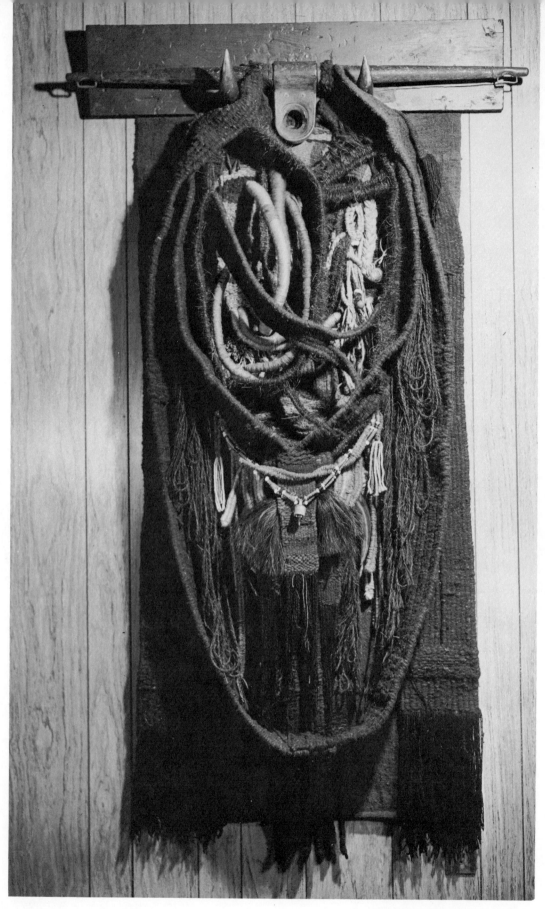

TAURUS. Dorothy Riley. 6 feet
high, 3 feet wide, 6 inches deep. An
old board and horns hold this rich
sculptural fiber form of woven,
wrapped, and braided wool and
some horsehair. Opposite:
TAURUS (detail). *Courtesy, Artist.*

WOVEN WALL #76. Olga de
Amaral. Colombia. 157 inches high,
79 inches wide. Braided and woven
horsehair and wool. *Courtesy,
"Deliberate Entanglements," UCLA.*

FLOOR TUBES. Shirley Fink. 2-1/2 feet high, 8 feet wide, 2 feet deep. Five cylinders were bolted together and used as the warp. Just enough room was left between the cylinders to pass the sisal weft through. A web of jute macramé across the top served as the foundation for innumerable jute cords tied on. Ends are unplied. *Courtesy, Artist.*

UNTITLED. Sharon Sulentor. 5-1/2 feet high, 4-1/2 feet wide. Braided rope, silk, polyester threads, and cotton threads twisted with nylon string. *Courtesy, Artist.*

8 Primitive Weaving and Braiding

Finger weaving and braiding are among many primitive techniques used by man for countless centuries. They probably predate loom weaving in the ancient world; the resulting fabrics were used for shelter and clothing. Among the Indians both finger weaving and braiding were used extensively for belts, ornamental sashes, and tumplines, which were worn around the waist, shoulders, arms, legs, and head.

For many years, weavers used braiding methods for tying off warps on a blanket or rug edge, and the practice is still popular. Now, braiding has proven adaptable for producing fabrics on a large scale for contemporary wall hangings; it also can be readily and brilliantly used to complement other weaving projects.

To begin finger weaving, several threads are tied together or clove hitched to a rod. One thread, which is longer than the others, is carried back and forth throughout the work and is used as a weft. The other threads are actually the warp.

The braiding illustrated is usually referred to as Osage braiding, although some books refer to it only as Indian finger weaving. In the Osage braiding technique, weaving proceeds in either or both of two ways: it can be worked from the center outward or from the outer threads to the center. No extra warp is introduced as in the finger weaving described previously. Each thread is suspended from a rod, and the threads are interwoven with one another in a one-over, one-under progression; each warp in turn becomes a weft. The outside threads are always brought back into the center as braiding continues.

In finger weaving and braiding, definite patterns can be established and followed for color and texture; or one can let the colors fall where they may for a random appearance. Weavings can be made in monochromatic or multicolored schemes.

FINGERWEAVING. Barbara Wittenberg. 12 feet high, 5 feet wide. The Osage braiding technique was used in the center section; fingerweaving with an auxiliary weft was used for the outer panels. Materials are white rope and black horsehair with clove hitching over the supporting and shaping rods. *Courtesy, Artist.*

For a fingerweaving sampler cut nine lengths of warp threads: five in one color and four in another. Cut one more thread twice as long as the others to use as the weft. Alternate the colors and place the weft thread on one side. Tie all the threads together in an overhand knot or clove hitch them to a dowel, pencil, or other holding device. Separate the longer weft thread from the warps. The warp ends hang loose. Hold the two colors of the warps separate so that you can pass the weft back and forth between the shed. Your fingers will act as the shed stick. You will have to change the weaving from one hand to the other as you work. Continue the process until the weaving is finished. Increase by adding doubled threads in the center or on the ends; decrease by weaving two threads together.

Fingerweaving in process. Mary Baughn. A wide hanging with many additions, slits, colors, and shapes. Observe how the yarns are wound into butterflies to prevent tangling. A paper underneath marked off into 1-inch squares helps to keep the work even.

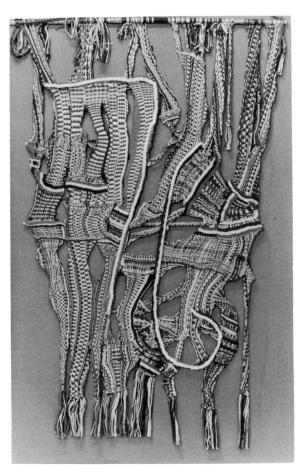

RED, WHITE, BLUE. Mary Baughn. 42 inches high, 25 inches wide. An ambitious fingerweaving project is supported with cloth-covered wire for an armature.

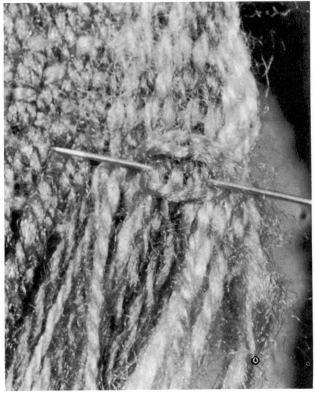

To hold one section of the work while you proceed in other areas, place a long nail (those used for trussing turkeys are good) in the shed. Wrap the weft around the nail so that it will be easy to pick up again.

OSAGE BRAIDING

The Osage braid technique, like fingerweaving, uses loose end warps that are interwoven. However, in braiding, each warp also becomes a weft. (In fingerweaving an extra length of thread is used as a continual weft throughout the work.)

To begin, mount the threads at the top by clove hitching to a rod, buckle, or grouped overhand knot. Here, a twining thread around each of the warps separates them and makes weaving easier, but any method will work. You could pass a weft through them, pin them individually, or develop any other system. The weaving begins at the center with one thread from each side crossed over and woven in and out of the threads on the opposite side. The next two adjacent threads in the center are then woven across the opposite sides until all the warps on one side cross over all on the other side.

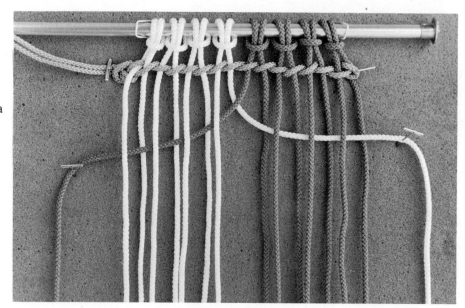

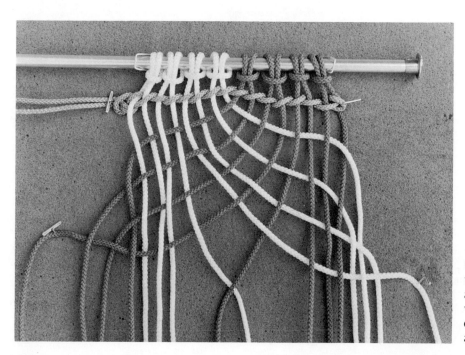

Each center thread that is brought to the outside is extended vertically and reworked into the following woven rows. Osage braiding also can begin with the outside threads and be worked toward the center.

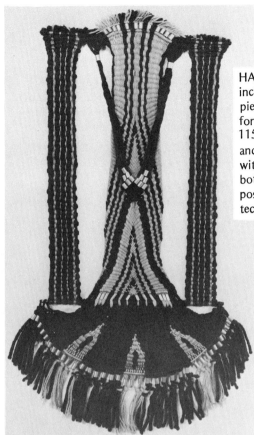

HANGING. Barbara Wittenberg. 36 inches high, 17 inches wide. This piece was originally the maquette for the 12-foot hanging on page 115. Osage braiding in the center and fingerweaving on the outside with the semicircle tabby at the bottom illustrate the variations possible by combining the techniques. Metal beads are added.

Assorted braided sashes. Suellen Glashausser. *Courtesy, Artist.*

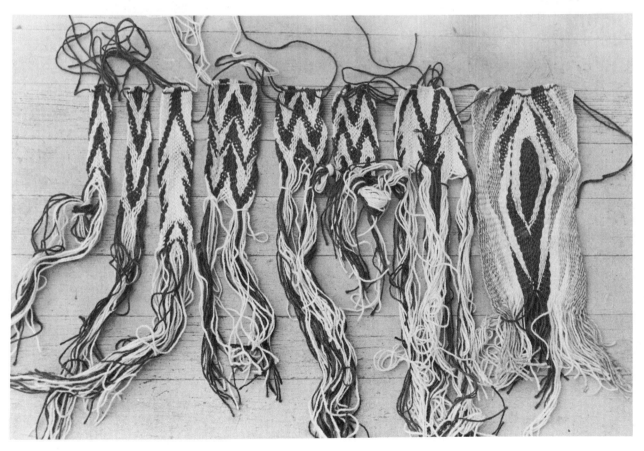

TOWER OF FLINTS. Gwynne Lott. 12 feet high. Made with twining and Mexican double braiding, a process similar to Osage braiding except that multiples of the threads are first woven into small diamond shapes. Then the shapes are woven together. Therefore, within the width of the weaving, you will have several centers or panels of braiding. *Courtesy, Artist.*

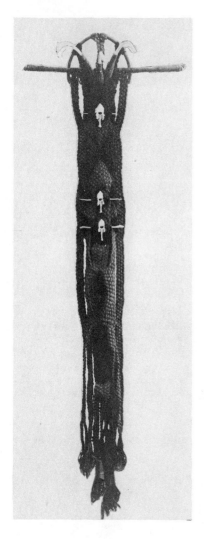

TOWER OF FLINTS (detail). Gwynne Lott. Jute upholstery dyed red and black. Bones are added by twining and wrapping.

LARGE YELLOW MASK. Suellen Glashausser. 3 feet high, 2 feet wide. Ghiordes knots woven into the warp were very long to allow ample ends for the fingerwoven hanging panels. Some braiding is added. *Courtesy, Artist.*

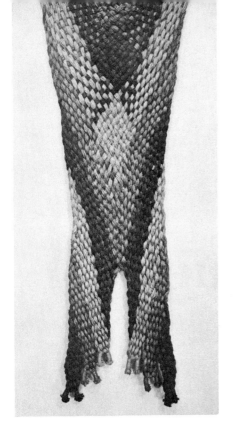

RED, BLUE, AND GREEN. Leslie G. Bohnenkamp. 10 feet high, 5 feet wide. Osage braiding with wrapped endings. Dyed sisal twine composed of 48 warps. *Courtesy, Artist.*

PINKS. Leslie G. Bohnenkamp. 4 feet high, 3 feet wide. Sisal dyed in different intensities of pink. A portion of the double piece at top was pulled through to the back of the work and woven separately in the back. The other warps were brought together, thus narrowing the width of the piece. The rear flap was brought through to the front at the bottom of the hanging and allowed to extend longer than the rear panel. *Courtesy, Artist.*

YELLOW. Leslie G. Bohnenkamp. 10-1/2 feet high, 4 feet wide. Sisal dyed yellow. The four pockets can be pushed in, as at top, or pulled out, as shown in lower portion. The bottom is finished by wrapping and unplying the twine. *Courtesy, Artist.*

121

9 Lace As an Off-Loom Technique

Many contemporary weavings contain motifs that are adaptations of lacemaking. Knotless netting (Chapter 11) is a modern interpretation of one type of needle lace. Bobbin lace, also called pillow lace, is another example of the renaissance of ancient techniques. Believed to have been born in sixteenth-century Genoa, bobbin lace eventually spread throughout Europe and evolved into a variety of traditional patterns associated with different countries.

The names "bobbin lace" and "pillow lace" derive from the fact that the lace is worked with bobbins while it is secured to a pillow. You can use a piece of polyfoam for a pillow until you learn how to do the braids and patterns. When you gain a little experience, attach threads to your weaving and work the braids and patterns directly. You can also braid the warps at the end of a weaving in the bobbin lace manner.

Bobbin lace is simple, and the results are elegant. There are only two basic movements, a twist and a cross, which are accomplished by moving two or four bobbins over one another. By interworking several pairs of bobbins, the wider patterns result. By varying the number of twists between a cross, the lace pattern changes.

Finely sanded, well-turned bobbins can be purchased from sources listed in the back of the book, or you can make some yourself from ¼-inch dowel cut into 5-inch lengths and notched about ¼ inch from one end. Bobbins should be sanded smooth so threads do not catch.

Traditional lacemaking utilizes set patterns with such names as torchon, net, and linen, to name a few. But one need not adhere to traditional patterns; it is more innovative and flexible to begin the crosses and twists in a free style and develop your

The setup for bobbin lace is shown in a sampler for the net ground pattern. Pairs of bobbins are twisted and crossed over each other to result in the braids. The ribbons stretched across the bobbins prevent them from tangling when they are not being worked. The work surface can be any soft pad into which pins can be placed firmly.

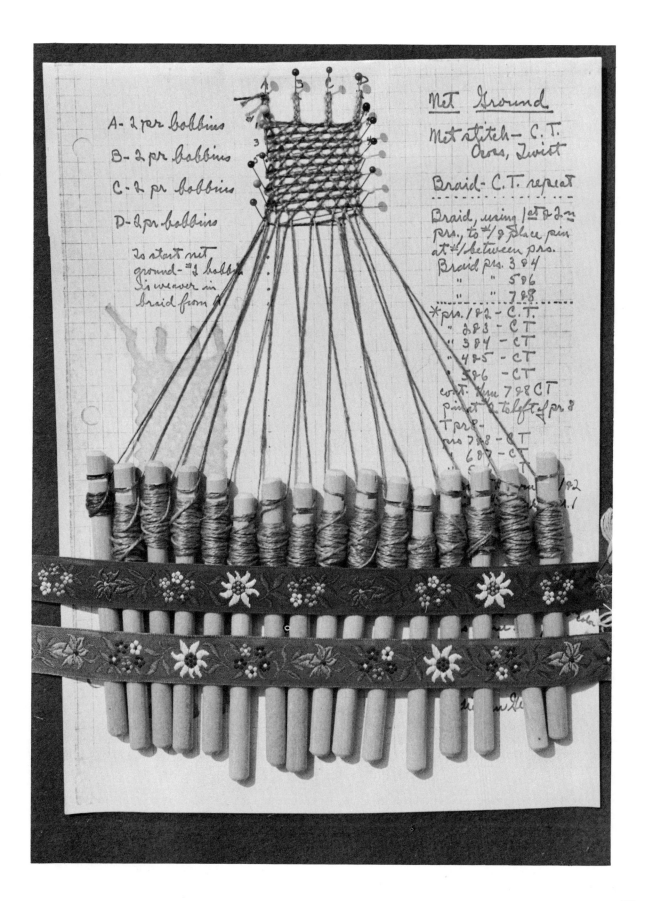

A- 2 pr. bobbins

B- 2 pr. bobbins

C- 2 pr. bobbins

D- 2 pr. bobbins

To start net ground- #1 bobbin is weaver in braid from

Net Ground

Net stitch- C.T.
    Cross, Twist

Braid- C.T. repeat
- - - - - - - - - - - -
Braid, using 1st & 2nd prs. to #/9 place pin at #/ between prs.
Braid prs. 3 & 4
  "   "   5 & 6
  "   "   7 & 8
- - - - - - - - - - - -
*prs. 1 & 2 - C.T.
  " 2 & 3 - CT
  " 3 & 4 - CT
  " 4 & 5 - CT
  " 5 & 6 - CT
cont. thru 7 & 8 CT
pin at 2 to left of pr 8
↑ prs.
prs. 7 & 8 - CT
  " 6 & 7 - CT

own patterns. The same is true of needle laces, which progress by interlacing the threads with a needle but in more randomly developed designs than the over and under progressions of weaving.

Fibers adaptable to lace methods are traditionally linen and cotton, but those already recommended for weaving and other off-loom techniques may be used. Heavier threads may require larger bobbins. Additional lace patterns can be found in *The Encyclopedia of Needlework,* by Therese De Dillmont, and the *Anchor Manual of Needlework.*

Traditional bobbin lace designs are developed into a contemporary shape. This small hanging, from an Israeli lacemaker, uses only crossovers and twists of the bobbins in a specific progression for each pattern. *Collection, Lee Erlin Snow.*

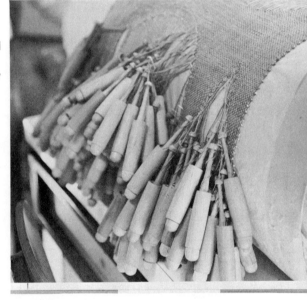

A lace panel in progress is worked around a large pillow with many pairs of bobbins. *Photo, Lee Erlin Snow.*

A lacemaker working with her bobbins. *Photo (taken at a lacemaking class in Jaffa, Israel), Lee Erlin Snow.*

Bobbin lace in a nontraditional design. Lydia Van Gelder.

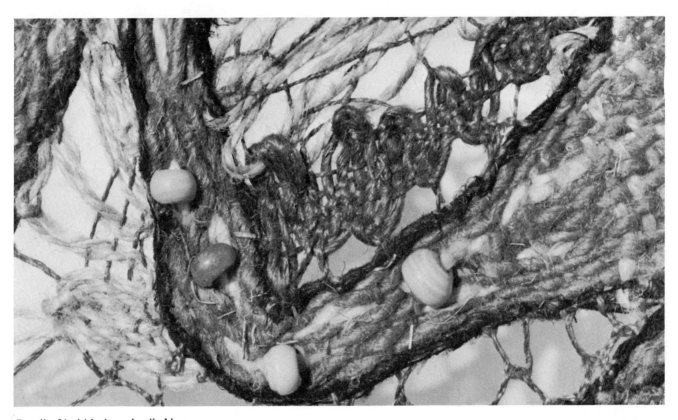

Detail of bobbin lace. Lydia Van Gelder. Beads and a variety of textured cords add to the visual excitement of the piece.

A lacemaker's pillow from Sweden is a padded muff shape set into a frame. A ratchet permits the pillow to be turned as the lace progresses so that the work does not have to be removed and repinned. *Photo, Roger Van Gelder.*

WEAVING OFF-LOOM

To prepare the bobbins for braiding: fold a length of thread in half and make a slip knot at the center and pin to board. This locates the center of the cord so that you will have an equal length of thread wound on each bobbin. Two pairs of threads (four bobbins) are required for each braid pattern.

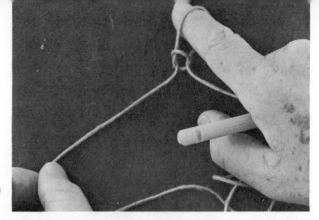

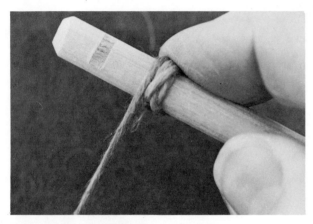

Begin to wind the thread by overlapping the bottom wind and winding the thread to the tip, allowing about a 4-inch working length.

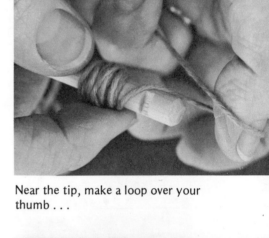

Near the tip, make a loop over your thumb . . .

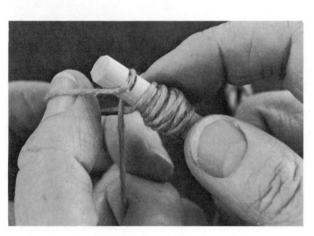

. . . and half hitch the cord onto the notch.

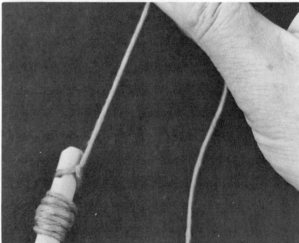

Pull to tighten.

When both cords are wound, remove the slip knot at the center. The setup should look like this.

When you begin braiding and extra thread is required, undo the half hitch, unwind the necessary length, and make another half hitch.

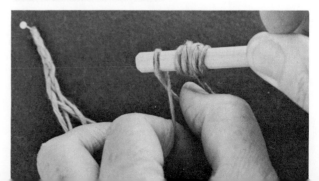

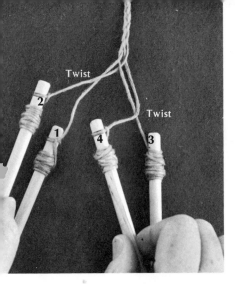

Patterns are made using only two hand movements with two pairs of bobbins, one pair in each hand. The hand position is important. For the twist: the right bobbin in each pair is passed over the left bobbin within each pair . . .

. . . and pulled to effect a twist in each pair of threads.

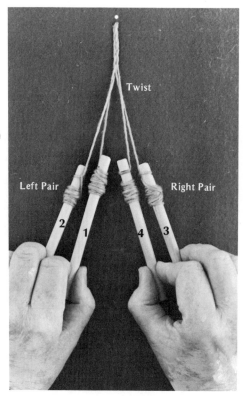

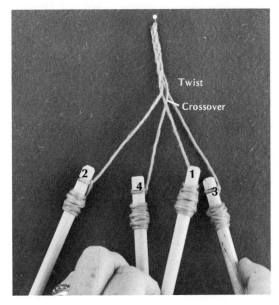

For the cross: the resulting *right hand* bobbin of the left pair is crossed over the *left bobbin* of the right pair. If you lose track, remember that it is the *under* thread of the left pair that crosses the *over* thread of the right pair.

Pull tight for the basic braid.

The work proceeds by holding a pair of bobbins in each hand and picking up and setting down the bobbins as needed. When more than two pairs of bobbins are used, number the pairs from left to right 1, 2, 3, 4, 5, etc. Then work pair number 2 over pair number 1; pair 3 over pair 2; pair 4 over pair 3; and so forth. Use other progressions to create different patterns.

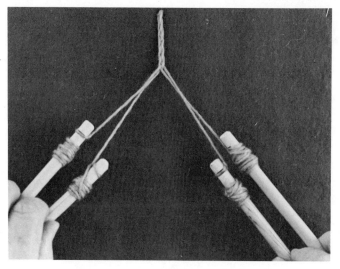

Patterns can be drawn on paper.
Then the twist and crossings with
the bobbins are developed to
duplicate the pattern. Lydia Van
Gelder.

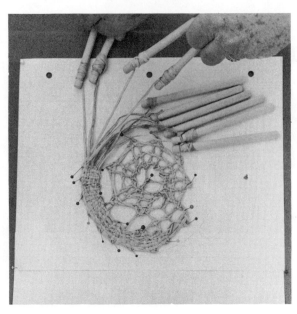

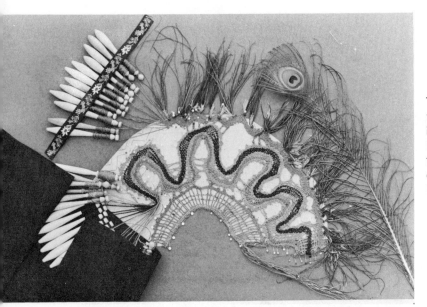

This weaving, in progress, is pinned
to a felt-covered Celotex board. It
is done in 10/2 linen and
incorporates strands from peacock
feathers for the endings. The
complete piece will be a necklace.
Lydia Van Gelder.

Ideas for lace woven patterns can
be observed in the stone carvings of
many buildings: this one, from the
Alcazar, Spain.

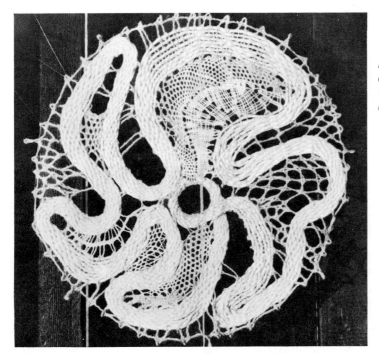

A round lace weaving with mixed designs in loose and tight weaves. Lydia Van Gelder. 21 inches in diameter.

Details of a round lace weaving illustrate the possible variations with the two basic movements intertwined. Several pairs of bobbins are used. All pieces by Lydia Van Gelder.

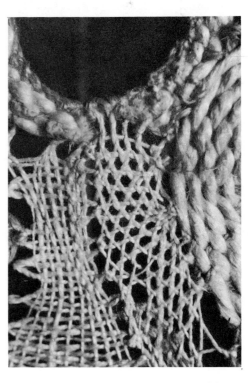

MOBILE. Lydia Van Gelder. 10 inches high. Bobbin lace using linen and Swisstraw with feathers and worked into a sculpture. *Photo, Roger Van Gelder.*

LACE WEED. Lydia Van Gelder. 36 inches wide, 12 inches high. Bobbin lace woven in a contemporary design. The lace was worked over a copper wire structure to give it stability. *Photo, Roger Van Gelder.*

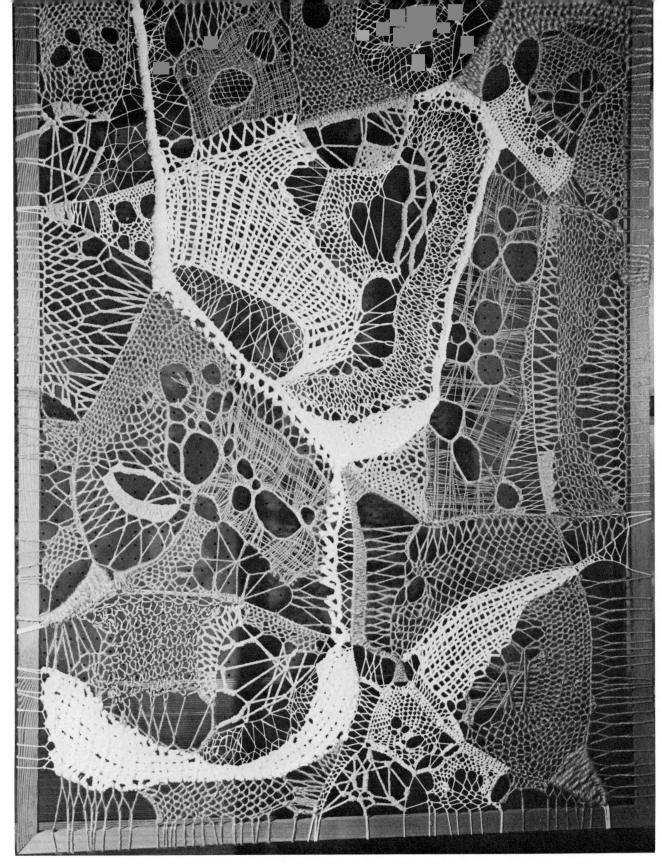

WEB IV. Evelyn Svec Ward. 54
inches high, 40 inches wide. A
hanging panel using needle lace
techniques, weaving, and knitting
with sisal, chenille wool, linen,
cotton, mixed threads, and
distorted burlap in naturals and
whites. *Photo, William E. Ward.*

TO TOUCH. Virginia Bath. 40
inches high, 62 inches wide. Needle
lace and machine lace with
embroidery. Used are linen, wool,
silk, mohair with mica, wood, brass,
ceramic ornaments, and amethysts.
Courtesy, Artist.

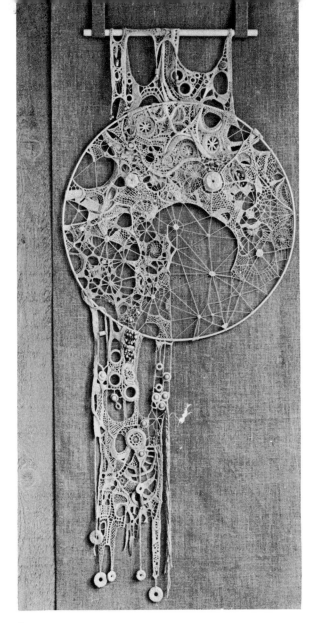

CRATERS. Virginia Bath. 12 inches in diameter. Needle lace. Linen, silk, and cotton with wood, brass, and wire. *Courtesy, Artist.*

FOAM. Virginia Bath. 48 inches high, 20 inches wide. Needle lace, machine lace, and embroidery. Natural and white on natural linen backing. Linen, cotton, and wool with wood, ceramics, and shells. *Courtesy, Artist.*

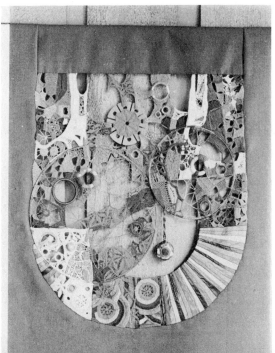

THE JOY OF ALEC'S GRANDMOTHER. Virginia Bath. 31 inches high, 25 inches wide. Needle lace and appliqué with wool, linen, silk, plastic, wood, and brass. *Courtesy, Artist.*

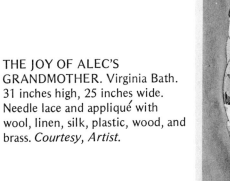

10 Spinning and Twisting Plies

Spinning is an activity that comes easily to most weavers. Transforming raw fleece into strands of wool is a satisfying, interesting activity. The textures and colors you can achieve by spinning, plying, and dyeing your own materials can add greatly to the way you feel about a finished weaving and its appearance. The beautiful hand-spun, thick-thin yarns lose the "perfect" quality of manufactured threads.

We normally think of spinning wool as coming from sheep, but many other kinds of hairs and fleece can be used: camel's hair, goat's hair, long dog hair, poodle and afghan hair, cotton, linen, and almost any material that can be teased, carded, and spun. After all, our ancestors have hand spun fibers for centuries. For the purpose of this discussion, however, we will deal with fleece from sheep because it is easiest to obtain and to spin.

Fleece is unspun wool. It can be purchased as it comes from the animal or after it has been cleaned and carded. It is sold by weight by weaving suppliers and ranchers in sheep-raising areas and from wool depots in many western cities. Ads for fleece can be found in the classified pages of weavers' magazines.

Fleeces differ greatly because animals and the climates in which they are raised differ. Sheep from cold climates have longer hair than those from warmer climates, and even the fleece from one sheep differs. The result is a vast variety in textures and qualities of spun wool.

Hand spinning is a simple procedure that requires a little practice. The number of photos used to describe the spinning process is to help you achieve proper results from the beginning. At first, and until you feel the rhythm of spinning, obtaining an even thread may seem elusive. But once you coordinate the twisting of the spindle in a clockwise direction with the right hand

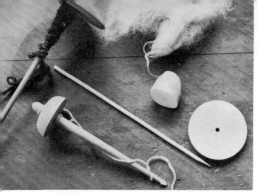

A spinning device can be composed of two parts: a long spindle and the whorl, which can be a wooden disc, a lump of clay, a half of a potato, or anything that will give momentum to the spindle when twirled between the fingers. You can make a spindle from a 3/8-inch dowel. Cut it about 12 inches long and notch it 1/2 inch from top. A yo-yo half can be used for the whorl.

PREPARING THE FLEECE
Raw fleece, as it comes from the sheep, has long, fibrous hairs that are matted together. These fibers must be pulled apart or broken down to be spun.

Breaking down these fibers is called *teasing* and *carding.* Teasing is achieved by pulling apart small sections of the fleece until the hairs within are evenly distributed. For more uniform preparation teasing, hand carder's, and carding machines are available from weaving suppliers. Carding puts the already teased fleece in order. Carding can be compared to brushing your hair.

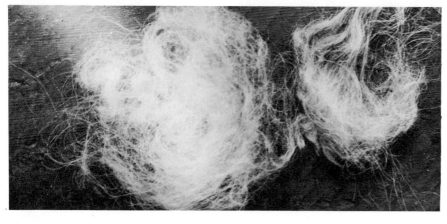

The clump at right is fleeced before it is teased or carded. The left clump shows the fleece after it has been teased. The hairs are relatively uniform and soft. The clump will be pulled into a long shape before it is spun.

while working the fleece with the left hand, you'll have little trouble. The result of spinning is a single-ply strand, which is wound onto the spindle to set the twist. When the spindle is filled, the yarn is wound off into a skein, washed and dried, and readied for dyeing or for use.

Fleece must be carded or teased before it is spun to make the fibers soft and even. Carding and teasing can be time consuming, so you may prefer to buy carded fleece that is already pulled into long sections. Fleece can be washed and dyed before spinning. This sometimes makes it a little harsh and difficult to spin, but it does yield nice variations of hues. If fleece dries out as a result of the washing processes, special oils can be added. A few drops of olive oil gently worked in with the hands will lubricate the fibers.

Anyone who plans to go into spinning thoroughly will discover a whole world of information. Start your investigation by contacting the sources for fleece and spinning information in the back of the book.

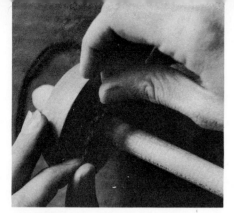

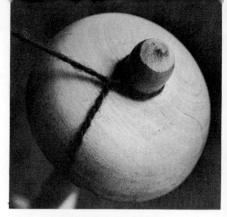

SPINNING

To spin, use about a 40-inch starting length of yarn attached to the fleece. Tie one end of the yarn onto the spindle and wrap it clockwise three times around the whorl.

Loop the yarn around the bottom of the spindle that comes through the whorl.

Make a half hitch to hold it.

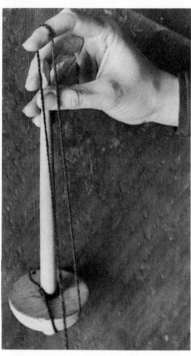

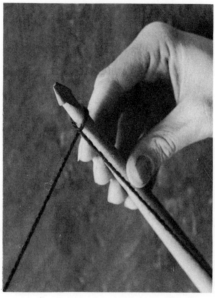

Bring the yarn up over the point of the spindle . . .

. . . and twist it.

The starting yarn, placed around the spindle, is now set up, and the fleece is ready for spinning.

Twist the spindle clockwise to begin spinning the fleece over the starting yarn. Your right hand will actively keep the spindle in a rhythmic clockwise motion while the left hand holds the fleece over the yarn. Use the right hand to draw the fibers down and out from the left hand. This movement controls the thickness of the yarn being spun.

Place a small mass of teased fleece in your left hand and hold it between your thumb and forefinger. Lay the top end of the starting yarn over the fleece and under your thumb. Let the spindle and yarn dangle.

The initial spin will cause the fleece to begin winding around the yarn. If the fleece breaks, restart by pulling and twisting until it reconnects. As each clump of fleece is spun, add more fleece.

While the spindle is in motion, use your right hand to help draw the roving (fleece that is pulled into a long mass) to keep it in a shape for easy spinning.

As you feel the rhythm, pull the roving into longer pieces while the spindle turns. When correctly spun, the wool will be a thin, medium-weight, continuous yarn. At first the strand may be lumpy, but as you continue to practice, you will spin an even thread. If areas do remain lumpy and will not take the spin, they can be untwisted and drawn out as the yarn dries after it is washed. If you have trouble getting everything going at once and the spindle hits the floor, rest the spindle on the table or floor to arrest the spin. Remember that the clockwise turn twists the yarn; counterclockwise untwists it.

To hold the twist, it is easiest to spin while the fleece is "in the grease" (before it is washed) and to wind it around the spindle until the twist sets. As you spin, wind the yarn around the spindle, beginning at the base near the whorl, until the spindle is full. When filled, it must be unwound into a skein by wrapping it around the back of a chair or someone else's upheld hands. Tie the skein at a couple of places to keep the strands in order. Then wash the strands carefully.

TWISTING PLIES

A strand of single-ply spun wool or other fiber usually is not very strong. Therefore, the weaver may twist strands to result in a two-, three-, or greater ply yarn. The same twisting methods may be used to add plies to any cord, yarn, or string when you want to combine colors or work with thicker cords than those commercially available. The Schacht rope-making machine twists plies quickly and efficiently. Twisting can also be done by hand with two people.

Clamp the double-pole separator to a table with a C clamp. The length of the yarn between the separator and turner should be about a third longer than the length of the finished yarn desired. Tie one end of yarn to hook A. Bring yarn around side of post B and down between the poles to center hook C. Loop it around and back between the poles and around to right of pole D. Bring down and around hook C, back up and around poles D and B, to the left. Return to hook A and tie. If you want even thicker rope, wind additional strands in the same way. Be sure to tie yarns off on hook A at the end.

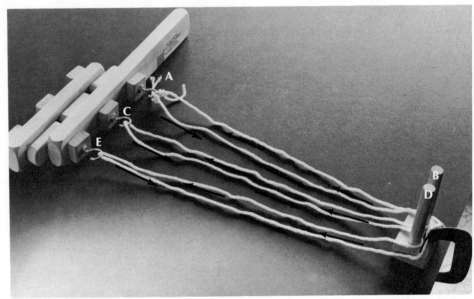

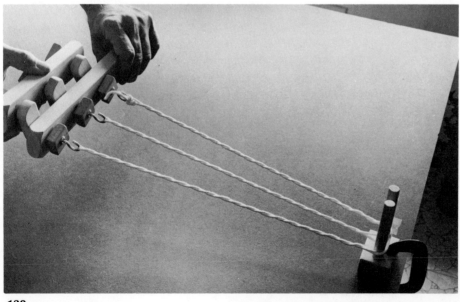

Keep yarn taut and crank the turner in a clockwise direction. As the twist takes up some of the yarn length, bring the turner closer to the separator. Crank until there is some overtwisting. The more turns you make, the tighter the rope will be.

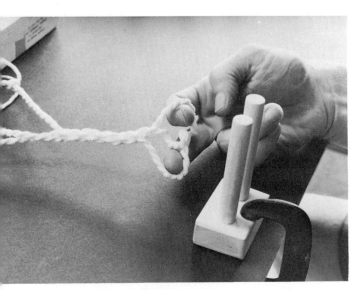

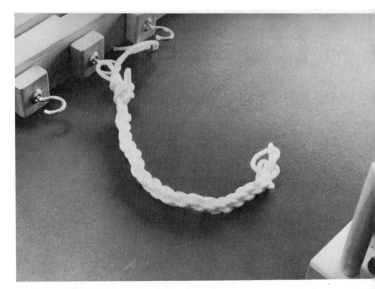

Now all the yarns on the separator should be twisted together. Grab the yarns behind the groove in the separator with two fingers. Remove the yarn and twist the three parts together in a counterclockwise direction until the full length of the rope is uniformly twisted.

For different colors, textures, and thicknesses, finished ropes are made from single-ply yarn wound into three plies and from preplied ropes.

Hold the rope tight and remove the yarns from the hooks. Tie ends together in an overhand knot to prevent them from unraveling.

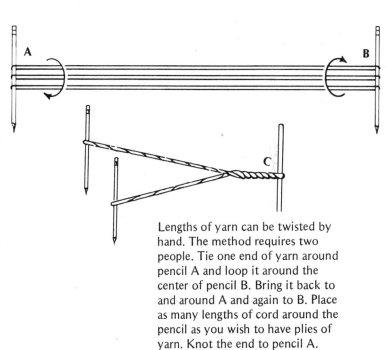

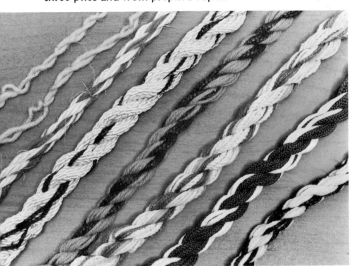

Lengths of yarn can be twisted by hand. The method requires two people. Tie one end of yarn around pencil A and loop it around the center of pencil B. Bring it back to and around A and again to B. Place as many lengths of cord around the pencil as you wish to have plies of yarn. Knot the end to pencil A. (The length of yarn between pencils should be three times the length of the finished cord.) Then each person twists the pencil in opposite directions, keeping the yarn taut. When the yarn begins to kink, hold the cord at the center C. Bring the pencils together and twist the two halves together. Remove pencils and tie cord ends together.

11 Knotless Netting, or Looping

Lacemakers of the Renaissance and eighteenth-century France, who looped thin threads over one another to produce the intricate patterns of the times, would be astonished to see what modern craftsmen have created using the same stitches. The work that is called "knotless netting" or "looping" by contemporary craftsmen is the same technique found in lacemaking books and called "needlemade" lace or "Renaissance" lace. This same technique was widely employed by American Indian tribes to produce loose, stretchy carrying bags, hairnets, nets, and other fiber objects. Canadian Indians made all kinds of items from leather strips.

The simple double looping of a thread over the loop of a previous thread may be accomplished with the thread held in your hand, by putting the strand through a needle, or around a bobbin. A needle is easier for looping thinner strands; the hands are best for heavier cords.

Knotless netting (to use the contemporary name) has emerged from the lacemaker's pillow and Indian idiom with explosive results. The forms include small, intricately patterned flat and relief surfaces, large bold hangings, sculptures, and complete environments. Often heavy ropes, yarns, stiff wires, and many other materials are combined.

The basic loops and variations for knotless netting are illustrated, but feel free to experiment with any twist and loop progression. The loops may be made loose, tight, or both, depending upon the purpose of the piece and the effect desired.

Although the demonstrations are illustrated on a horizontal holding cord, the same method can be developed over a warp, weft, or an object to make different shapes and textures. You also can create a piece in knotless netting first, and then use other fiber techniques on top of it.

OUTDOOR ENVIRONMENT. Barbara Schawcroft and students. Fibers were strung about in the courtyard of the Yarn Depot, San Francisco, during a seminar on knotless netting. Yarns and ropes of various colors and textures were looped onto the open and closed areas. Observe how the technique can result in loose- and tight-woven sections. *Photographed at the Yarn Depot, San Francisco.*

As you work and learn what the loops look like, you'll be able to recognize knotless netting in many pieces throughout the book and in new works being shown in textile exhibits. You also will be able to identify the knotless netting technique in historical examples of laces, basketry, weaving, and so forth, and will be able to adapt the variations to contemporary statements.

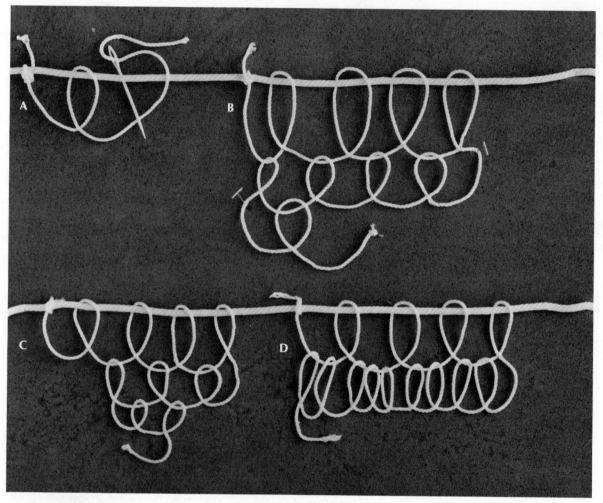

A) Pin a holding cord across your board or in a frame. Tie your working thread to the holding cord. To loop, bring the working thread over the holding cord, swing to the left and under the holding cord and over the first part of the working cord. Continue making these loops for as long an area as you like.

B) To reverse, pin the cord to the board; then loop the second row over the bottom loop of the previous row.

C) To decrease, omit working into the end loop or anywhere in the center.

D) To increase, place two or more loops on the curve of the loop in the previous row.

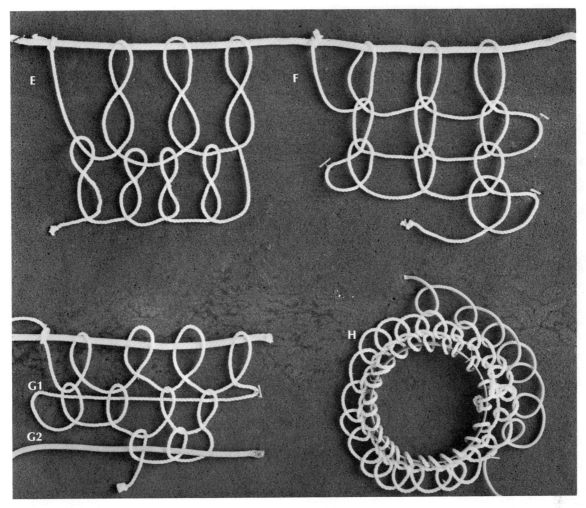

VARIATIONS

E) The figure 8 is a variation of the loop. Twist the working thread into a figure 8 before bringing it around to the next loop. Rows are increased or decreased as with single looping.

F) Overlooping. Instead of attaching the rows to the curve of the loop, loop over the cross of the previous row, as shown.

G) Horizontals can be added along with the looping using the same working cord, as in row G1, or by adding an independent thread, as in row G2. Use this method when adding onto warps or wefts of a weaving.

H) Knotless netting also can be worked over a rod, a ring, or other nonflexible holding lines. If loops formed tend to be uneven, place a ruler or other stick under the loops. Colors can be added at will, and threads can be tied together. Loose ends can be tied together or worked into the composition at the back, or they can be emphasized and made part of the composition. (For additional looping ideas refer to deDillmont's *Needlemade Laces.*)

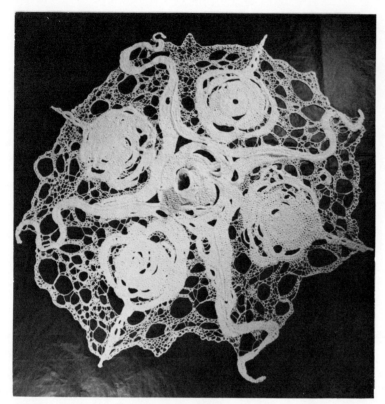

OCTOPUS. Janet McNinch. 70 inches in diameter. A round linen and raw silk tablecloth of knotless netting as lace in a contemporary adaptation. The four-place-setting is started as a single crocheted chain onto which the netting is looped. A crocheted edge also forms the center backbone, or ridge, in the tentacles of the octopus and outlines the scallops of the seashell shape. Otherwise, the entire piece is knotless netting. *Photo, Edwin McNinch.*

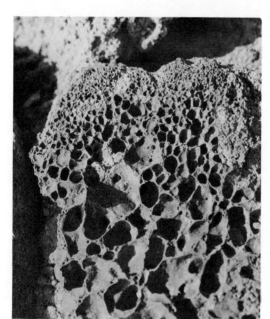

Patterns in fossilized rock photographed close up in a wall in Pompeii, Italy, can suggest texture for compositions of knotless netting, crochet, weaving, and mixed techniques.

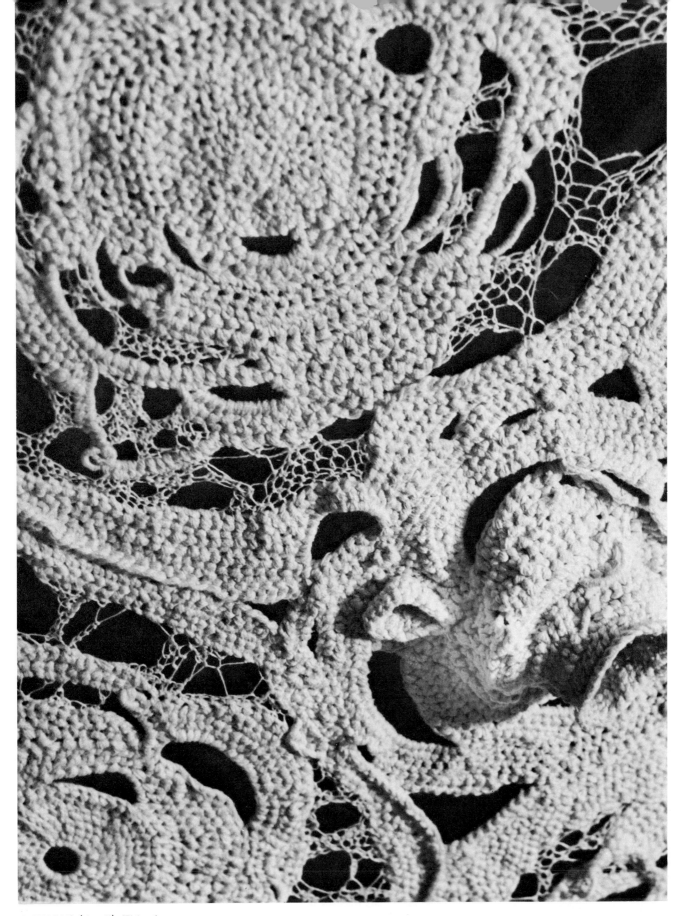

OCTOPUS (detail). This piece
illustrates the appearance that can
be obtained by loose or tight
looping.

Knotless netting, also referred to as needlemade lace, is the inspiration for this unusual composition, by Tina Krythe. Loops are made over warps and wefts around a frame (below) using the front and back threads on the frame separately and together. When finished, another frame was placed over the lower frame for the final presentation.

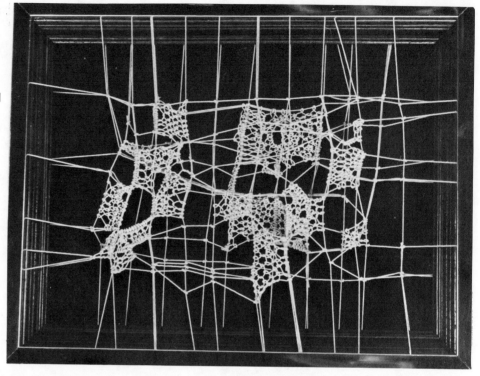

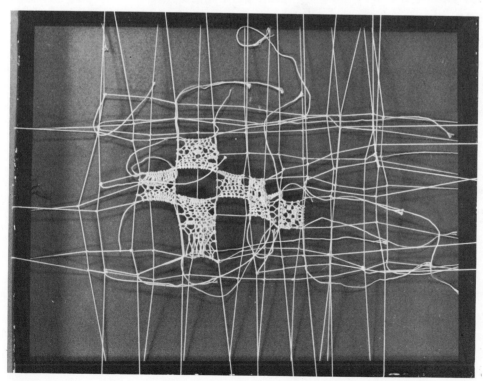

A picture lace composition in work. Tina Krythe. Cords are warped around the frame and looped around one another at several junctions to hold them in place. The looping proceeds with a needle or the fingers. Looping can progress horizontally or vertically. It can be worked between cords on the front layer, on the back layer, or both. The possible effects are infinite in variety.

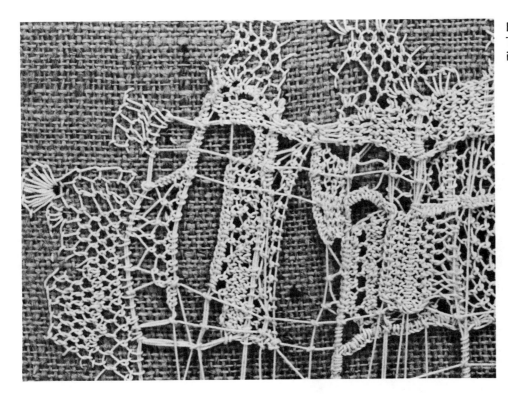

KNOTLESS NETTING (detail).
Tina Krythe. 8 inches high, 10
inches wide.

Needle looping is used for the main
design. Done with a needle and
thread simultaneously sewn through
the burlap and thread warps.

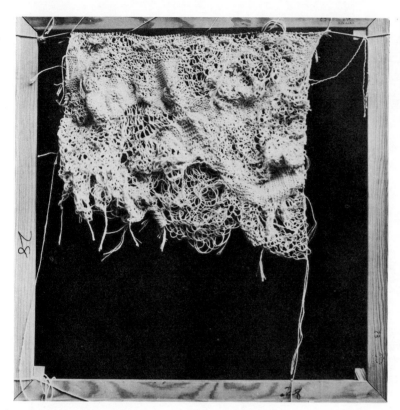

PUNTO IN ARIA. Joanne Brandford. Knotless netting, in progress, is worked on a frame. To prevent the finished work from curling, the artist added a glass rod at the bottom. *Courtesy, Artist.*

The swirling design, subtle color variations, and sweep of knotless netting suggest a feeling that can be compared to waves washing on shore.

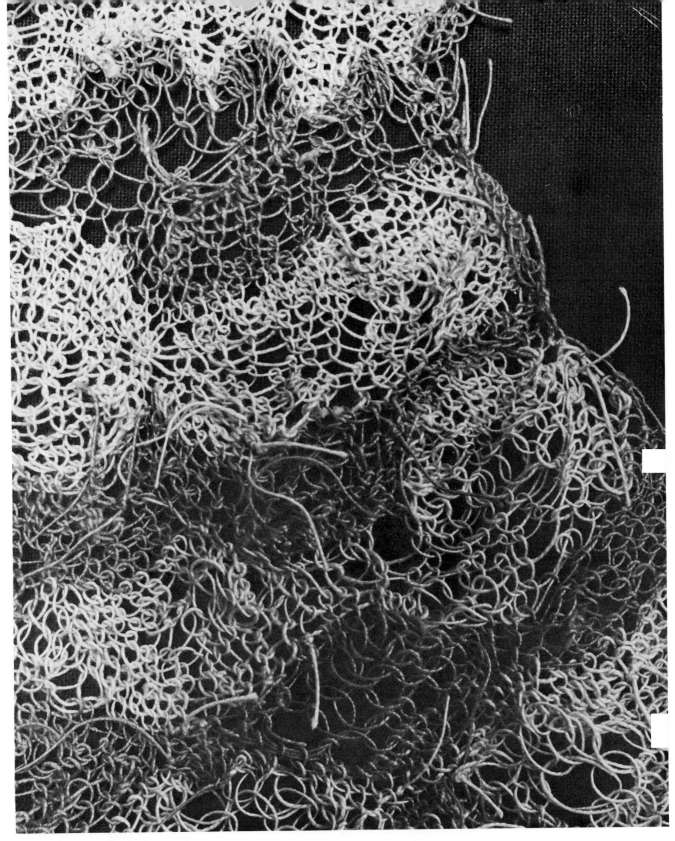

ADJUA'S BIB. (detail). Joanne
Brandford. The massing of loops,
some over the bar of the previous
row, some behind the cross-over of
the other, some tight, some loose,
some darker than others, shows the
variations possible for patterning
and texturing a composition in this
technique. *Courtesy, Artist.*

149

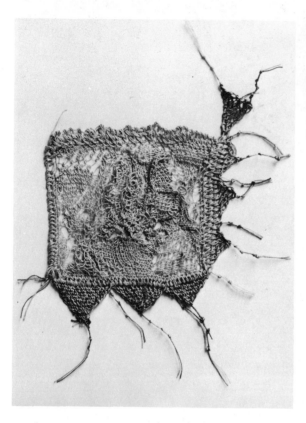

KASHIWA. Joanne Brandford. 4 inches high, 5 inches wide. Knotless netting worked on a small embroidery hoop with a needle illustrates how panels can be added and how readily the shapes can be decreased and increased. *Courtesy, Artist.*

ADJUA'S BIB. Joanne Brandford. 9-1/2 inches high, 7-1/2 inches wide. The piece was developed on an embroidery hoop. The finished piece was mounted on a frame under glass. *Courtesy, Artist.*

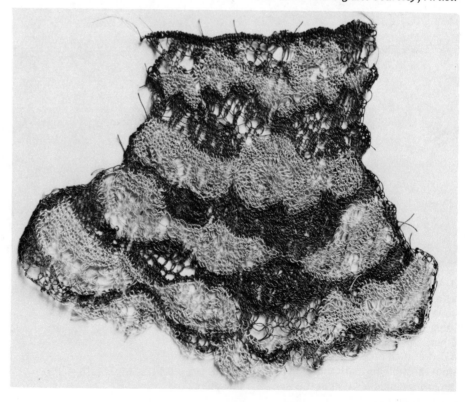

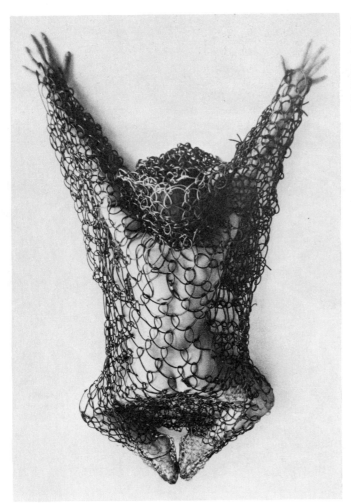

A FIBROUS RAIMENT. Debra E. Rapoport. 5-1/2 feet high, 5 feet wide. Constructed in knotless netting of amber plastic tubing and plastic-coated copper wire. It is stretchable, so it will fit and adapt to the body. *Photo, Demetre Lagios.*

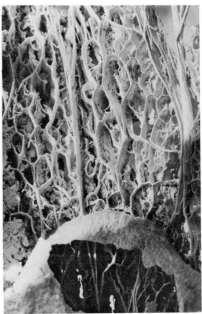

Try using this highly magnified plant form to suggest directions for knotless netting compositions. Use it vertically or horizontally.

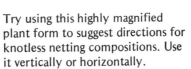

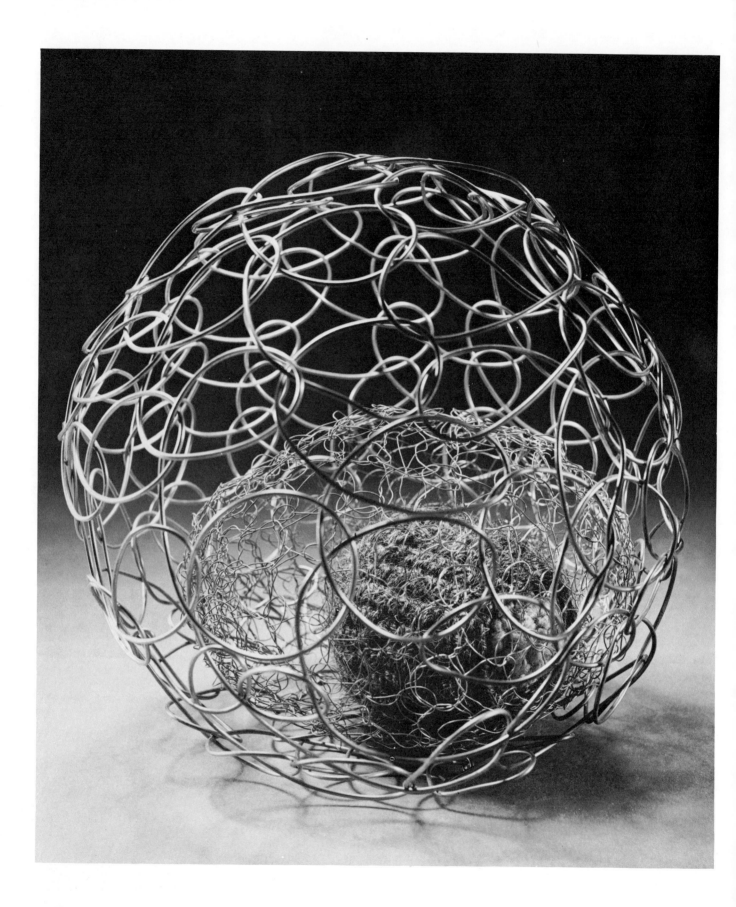

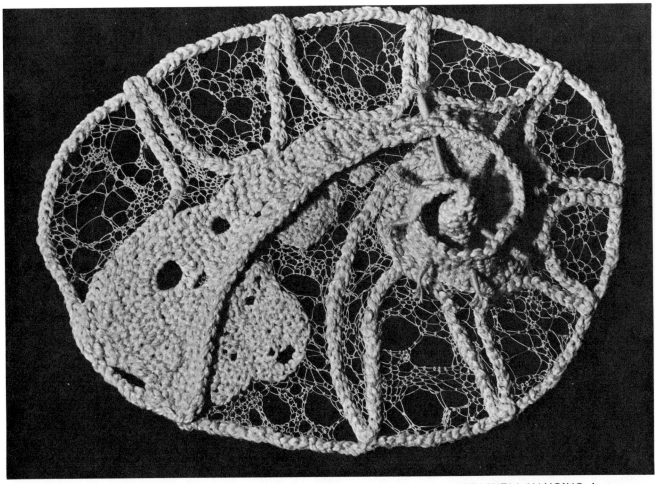

SEASHELL HANGING. Janet McNinch. 30 inches high, 40 inches wide. Mainly knotless netting with crocheted edges and outlining. Heavy cotton, sisal, and linen are designed to capture the gesture of a seashell. Linen-wrapped dowels help to reinforce the three-dimensional center. *Photo, Edwin McNinch.*

SPHERICAL THREE-PART CONSTRUCTION. Judith I. Kleinberg. Outer shell approximately 8 inches in diameter. Made of brass and copper wire in knotless netting. The second shell, about 5 inches in diameter, is crocheted wire; the centermost form, 3 inches in diameter, is crocheted horsehair and jute. *Photo, Royal A. Lyons.*

MENEHUNE. Bea Miller. 5 inches high, 3-1/2 inches wide. The piece was started on the plastic rung at right. String and afghan hair. *Courtesy, Artist.*

KNOTLESS NETTING SCULPTURE. Phoebe McAfee. About 7 inches high, 10 inches wide. Waxed linen. *Photographed at the Yarn Depot, San Francisco.*

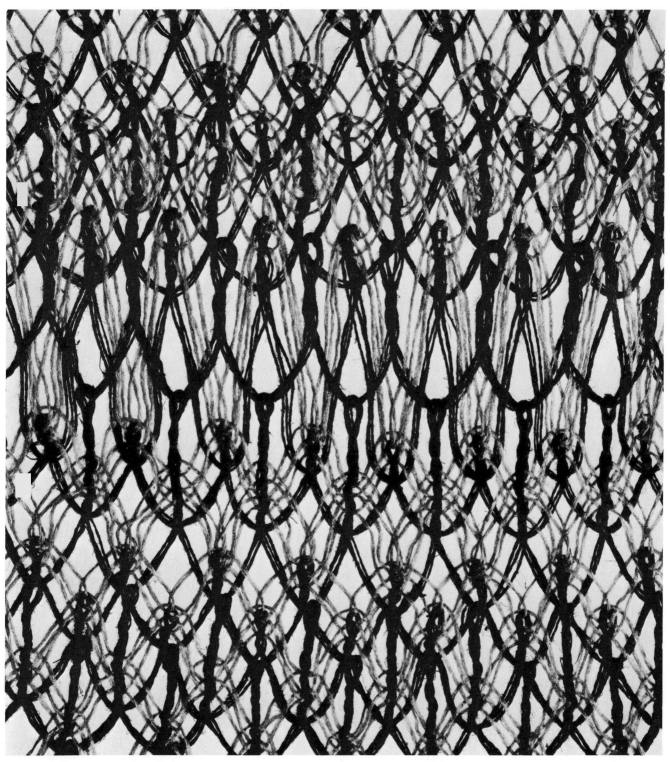

OPEN STREAM (detail). Evelyn
M. Gulick. The light-colored, thin
yarn areas are needle-weaving. The
twisted dark color cords are the
loops of knotless netting. *Photo,
Harry Crosby*.

12 Crochet

Crochet has found many exciting applications among serious artists as an expressive technique for creating highly individualized forms and as an adjunct to weaving, knotting, knitting, and other methods. Crochet can be considered an off-loom weaving technique because it involves interlacing of fibers using only a hook or the fingers. Knowing how to crochet expands the techniques at your fingertips and broadens the scope and direction of the forms you create. Throughout the book, examples that combine crochet with other techniques are described; observing their uses and combinations can stimulate ideas for you to apply.

Crochet hooks vary in size from a tiny metal eye-straining size to large plastic and wooden ones that may be an inch in diameter. You can fashion your own hook from a wood dowel, but it should be smoothly sanded to prevent yarns from catching.

Your fingers also can serve as a crochet hook. Yarns worked in a free-finger crochet manner can be combined with hooked crochet and other off-loom methods. The fingers reach through the loops in the same way as does the hook. They also can reach through holes in knitted, netted, and woven areas to bring yarns through so that they can be crocheted.

Crochet can be worked over hoops and found objects. It is not necessary to use traditional crochet yarns. Some of the most exciting crochet work is done with rope, rug yarns, weaving yarns, and anything that will adapt to a specific project.

The chain, single, double, and triple crochet are illustrated. With them, you have a basic approach that will take you through hundreds of creative hours. For other variations, refer to the scores of crochet books and instructions available in monthly magazines.

KING PHILLIP'S CASTLE. Audrey V. Sylvester. 9 feet high, 8 feet in diameter at bottom. A two-ply nylon teepee for two using finger crochet construction over guy wires, which were removed after crochet was finished. *Photo, Jack Adams.*

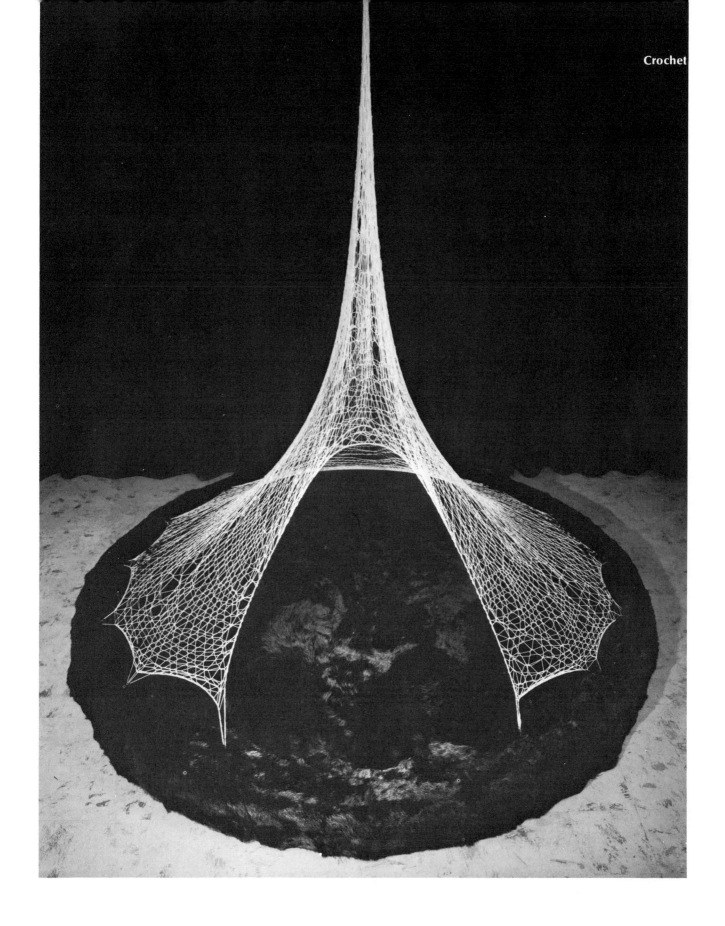

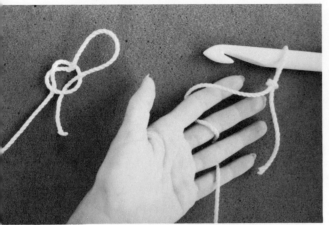

To crochet a foundation chain:
A) Make a slip knot about 6 inches from end of yarn. Insert hook in loop and pull one end of yarn to tighten knot. Place yarn around your finger to maintain tension.

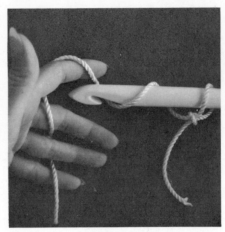

B) Place hook under and over yarn.

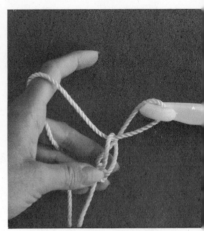

C) Catch yarn with hook and pull through the loop. Make chain as long as you like. To turn back, place hook in a loop of the chain and continue with the single crochet.

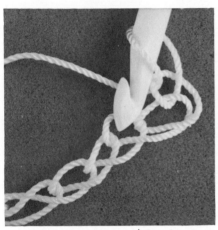

For single crochet: A) Retain one loop on the crochet hook. Place hook into second chain from hook.

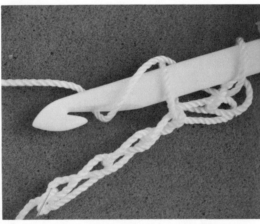

B) Loop hook under and over yarn.

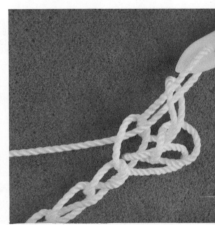

C) Catch yarn and pull through both loops.

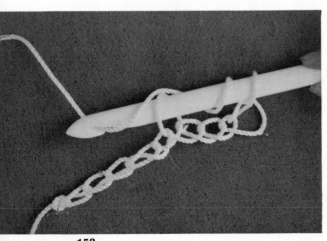

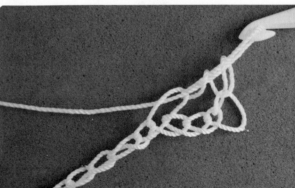

For double crochet: A) You have one loop on hook. Wind yarn over hook and put hook through fourth loop on chain. Yarn over hook again . . .

B) . . . and pull yarn through two of the three loops, yarn over hook again, and pull through remaining two loops.

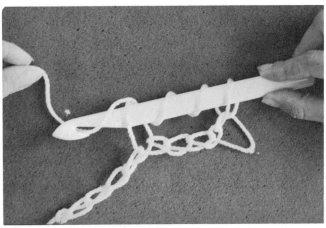

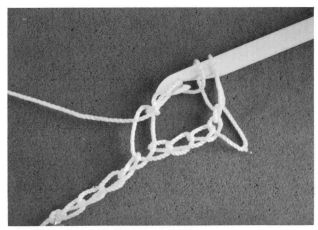

For triple crochet: A) Put yarn over hook twice. Insert hook into the fifth chain and draw up that loop. Put yarn over hook again.

B) Draw back through two loops only. (Two remain on hook.)

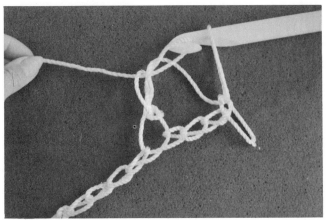

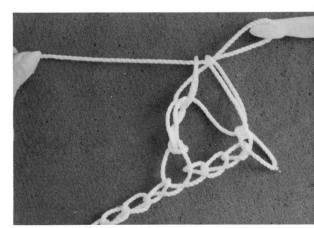

C) Put another yarn over the hook and draw through two loops only.

D) Put yarn over hook again and then through the last two loops — completing the triple crochet.

You can substitute your finger for a crochet hook. You use your thumb and finger to pick the threads through the loops. Finger crochet loops are large and can be combined with those made with the crochet hook when very loose weaves are combined with tighter weaves.

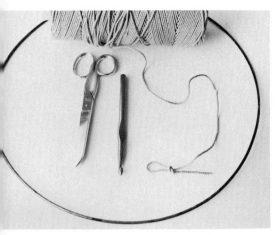

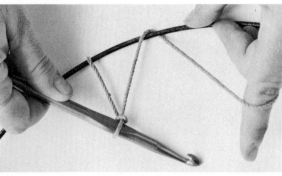

A) Insert the crochet hook into the slip knot and pass the yarn under the edge of the hoop before passing it around your hook.

B) Bring first loop next to hoop. Pass hook under and over yarn.

Many armatures are used to support a crocheted piece. The following is an excellent method for attaching crochet to a hoop or other object. You need only the object, a crochet hook, a pair of scissors, and yarn or string. Waxed linen cord is used here.

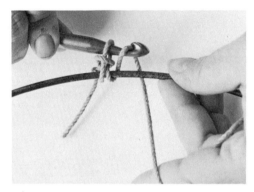

D) After you have completed the first loop, pass the yarn under the hoop and the hook under and over the yarn.

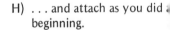

E) Pull the yarn through the loops in a continual single crochet. . .

C) Hook yarn and pull through loop. Be sure that the hook is beneath the hoop and the yarn, over.

G) A series of loops can be made around the wire. When you want to warp with a crochet chain, make a single foundation chain, pull it across the hoop . . .

H) . . . and attach as you did at beginning.

F) . . . and continue to work the loops around the hoop as far as you wish.

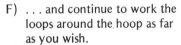

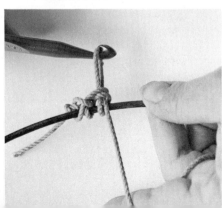

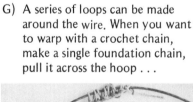

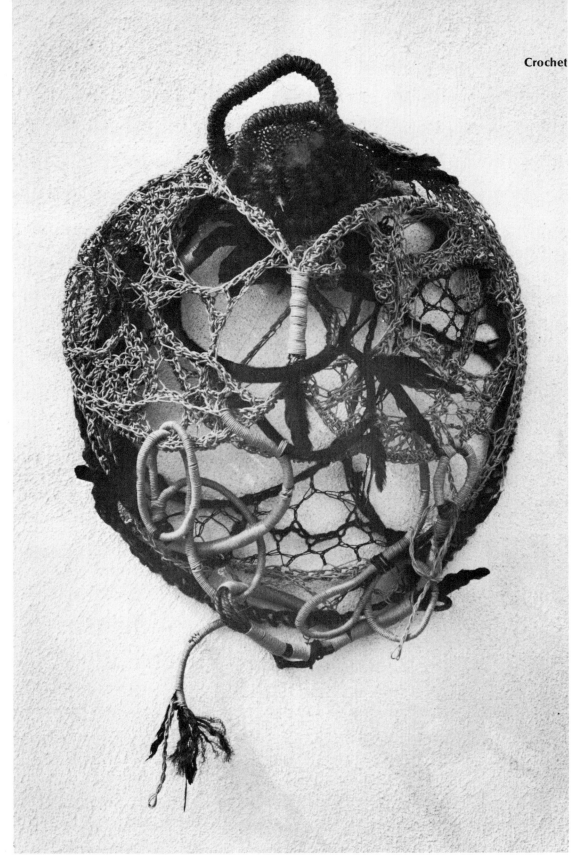

AMERICAN FETISH II. Lee Erlin
Snow. 30 inches in diameter. Metal
hoops are joined to create a
sculptural shape of waxed cord,
wool yarns, jute, and feathers.

AMERICAN FETISH I. Lee Erlin
Snow. 5-1/2 feet high. Six metal
hoops are joined to form a
three-dimensional wall-suspended
sculpture using crocheting,
wrapping, and knotting.
Detail on opposite page.

AMERICAN FETISH I (detail). Lee
Erlin Snow.

CROCHET SCULPTURE. Dolores
Fangon. 3 feet high. Goathair and
orlon yarn on wire armature.

SEA ANEMONE. Fern Miller. 7
inches high, 24 inches wide.
Driftwood, wool, and unspun
synthetic yarns using free crochet.
A deliberate interpretation of an
organic form.

The forms of a squid might have
been the inspiration for Dolores
Fangon's crocheted sculpture.

SHRINE #7. Walter Nottingham.
Crochet and weaving on an
armature. Wool, feathers, and beads.
Courtesy, Artist.

PER-CHIK-O-REE. Elisabet
Siewert-Miller. 18 inches in
diameter. Fur with crocheted wool.
Photo, Nickerson.

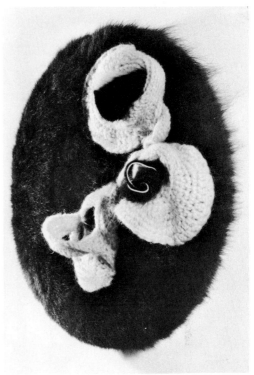

WALL HANGING. Sherry Cook.
10 feet wide. Stuffed crochet.
Courtesy, Artist.

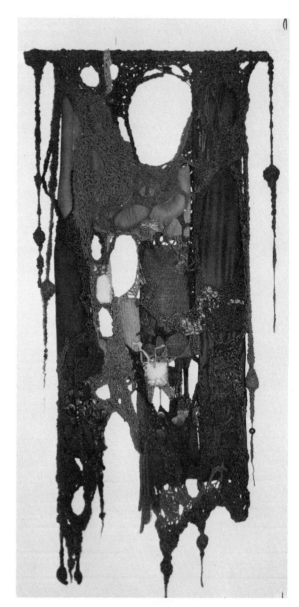

RED PADDED WALL HANGING.
Susan Lyttle. 60 inches high. A
patchwork of padded fabric pieces
sewn together by areas of weaving
and crochet. *Courtesy, Artist.*

CROCHET SCULPTURE. Jane
Knight. Approximately 5-1/2 feet
high, 12 inches in diameter. Round
shapes are held solid by clear plastic
circles in different widths. *Photo,
Richard Knight.*

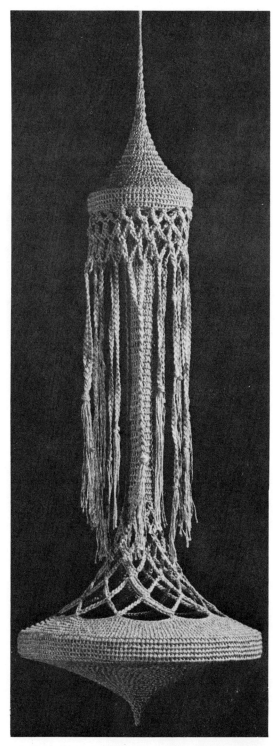

MAYTIME. Jane Knight. 6 feet high, 18 inches in diameter. Crocheted in brilliant-colored wools. *Photo, Richard Knight.*

GREEN KNIGHT. Walter Nottingham. Crochet and weaving. *Courtesy, Artist.*

WHITE FETISH. Susan H. Brown.
27 inches high, 10 inches wide.
Courtesy, Artist.

UNTITLED. Jane Knight. Crochet.
Photo, Richard Knight.

MASK. Susan Lehman. Crochet.
*Photographed at the Yarn Depot,
San Francisco.*

I AM EVERYTHING. Norma C. Minkowitz. 72 inches high, 24 inches wide. Free-form crochet, with weaving in and out of crochet surface. Hooking, appliqué, stuffed forms, and stitchery worked on a commercially woven fabric. *Courtesy, Artist.*

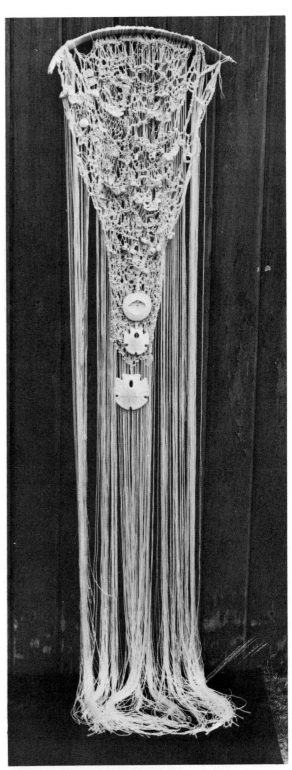

ODE TO A SEA BRIDE. Helen Richards. 58 inches long, 14 inches wide. Crochet and netting started on rib bone and worked down. Sand dollars and ceramic beads added.

ABOUT GRANDMOTHER
EMMIE. Mary Ventre. 29 inches
high, 27 inches wide. Crochet with
coat hanger armature. *Courtesy,
Artist.*

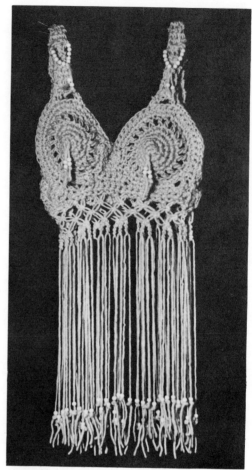

BAN THE BRA TOP. Bucky King.
Crochet and macramé with beads.
Courtesy, Artist.

CERAMIC AND FIBER
CONSTRUCTION #2. Judith I.
Kleinberg. Crochet fiber form is
hollow and enclosed except for one
ceramic opening. It maintains its
shape without stuffing. *Photo,
Royal A. Lyons.*

COAT OF ARMS. Blanche Carstenson. 16 inches high, 16 inches wide. Needle weaving with crochet.

GREEK BIRD. Martie Holmer. Crochet wings are combined with a twined top center section of wrapping and braiding over a curved iron rod. *Photo, Leslie Miller.*

13 Basketry Techniques

Basketmaking techniques developed centuries ago by our ancestors are emerging in new shapes and forms for contemporary baskets and sculptures. The techniques are being used by themselves and in conjunction with other weaving methods. Traditionally, we think of utilitarian basket shapes and designs so characteristic of certain countries and various cultures within a country that historians are able to date and place them. Future historians will have little trouble placing the baskets being made by today's artists because they are new and unique.

Contemporary baskets are made of fibers by themselves and in conjunction with traditional grasses. They are not necessarily utilitarian. Rather they are works of art that exploit the colors and textures of threads and ropes. They exist in space as sculptural forms, and some definitely move out of the basket category and into the area of sculpture. Often the parts of a basket are created separately and assembled to achieve a desired effect.

Basic basket techniques are coiling, twining, and weaving. Coiling is demonstrated in this chapter. Twining, already illustrated on page 34, can be adapted to basketmaking. A method for starting a twined basket from the top, rather than the bottom, is shown. A woven basket is begun in the same way you begin weaving on a circle (see page 80). Basket shapes also can be started over a cardboard, as shown on pages 67-68. Working the sides of the basket involves holding the warps in the position you want the shape to take.

The main problems in basketry involve finishing methods and maintaining a flat bottom. For finishing, ends are usually tapered and rewoven into the coil so they don't show, or they are deliberately increased and used for an aesthetic presentation. Beads, fringes, feathers, and other baubles may be added. Reeds

THREE CHIMNEYS. Marie Waters. 10 inches high, 5 inches in diameter. Coiled basket with crown of beads using a raffia coil covered with jute. The completed basket was dyed with walnut hull dye. *Courtesy, Artist.*

or rattan used as the base must be kept pliable by soaking them completely for six hours and then keeping them in water until ready to use. Yarns that are coiled, twined, or woven over wet reeds should be colorfast since the structure must be re-wet frequently.

For a coiled fiber base, use thick, heavy yarns such as sisal, several strands of jute, sea grass, gardener's rope, clothesline—anything that will hold the shape. Hold the coil flat as you work the bottom of the basket. Hanging forms also can be created and will serve to eliminate the flat bottom problem.

Two types of coiled baskets are shown. Left, the base cord shows, and the wrapping cord holds the coils together but does not cover them. The resulting structure is decorative but not solid. Right, the base coil cord is completely covered by the wrapping cord, which is brought from one coil over the next coil as the cord is wound into shape. By careful placement of the wrap cord over the coil a pattern results. Dona Meilach.

A finished coil base with free-form open-wrapped cords. Lee Erlin Snow.

A) Begin coiling at the bottom center of the basket. The end coil cord is tapered.

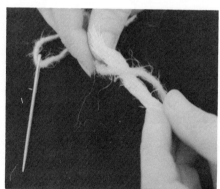

B) Begin wrapping with another cord threaded on a needle.

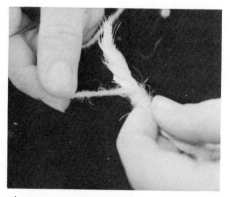

C) Wind the wrapping cord around the coil base about an inch from the tapered end.

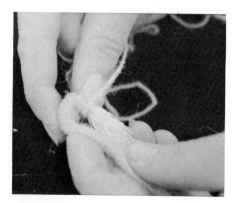

D) Bend the coil and . . .

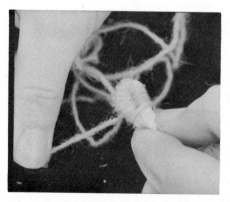

E) . . . wrap around to hold. Bend and create the center.

F) Put the needle through the center of the coil and continue winding and lacing the needle around each ring of coil as it develops. Do *not* keep bringing the thread to the center.

HATCHED EGG UNDER
BASKET. Virginia H. Barber.
Coiled basket shapes are combined.
Jute is used for the foundation, and
the jute is wrapped with wool
weaving yarns in blue-green, gold,
and rust. The egg was woven in two
parts, which were hinged about a
third of the way around. As the
work progressed, feathers were
added. The feathers were aimed in
the direction of the finished part of
the coil so that they would not be
in the way of the rest of the
wrapping. *Courtesy, Artist.*

SIDNEY. Lucele Coutts. 7 inches
high, 16 inches wide, 8 inches deep.
Rug wool on a jute foundation with
wooden beads and rya knots added.
Coiling can move in any direction.
Hold the foundation cord and
work it in the shape desired as you
wrap the coils. *Courtesy, Artist.*

Twining is used extensively for baskets because it completely covers the warp and results in a sturdy form that will retain its shape. Twined baskets can be started from the center base in the same way a weaving is begun (see twining, page 34). You can also begin the form from the top, as shown here.

Twined basket in progress. Fibers over reed warps. The shape was begun from the top. Finishing off bottom in this kind of shape is tricky and requires considerable experimentation. A coiled bottom may be set in, and a coiled lid may be added. To add cords to expand the shape, fold over an additional warp, add it between others, and twine the cords in consecutive order. To decrease, twine around two warps at once or drop one into the inside of the work where it won't show. *Photo, Lee Erlin Snow.*

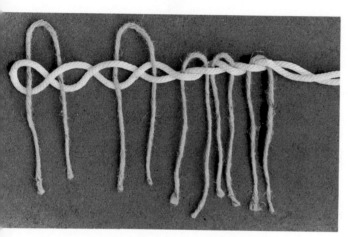

Use lengths of folded cord for the warp and twine the top row as shown.

To return for a second row, continue the twining in reverse direction, as illustrated.

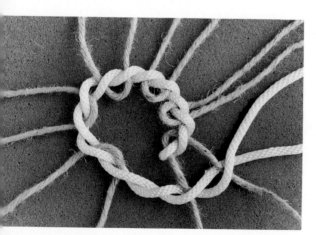

To connect the circle, lay the cords as shown and follow around.

Keeping the twined cords in order at the beginning can be confusing; therefore, holding the warps in the palm of one hand while twisting the weft with the other hand is practical. The warps can be pinned to a Styrofoam or cork board until there are enough rows to pick the work up and continue with it in your hands.

COW'S UDDER. Carol Shaw.
Twined basket begun at top uses
the warp endings in wrapped
shaping. A coiled bottom is added.
Top is crochet and coiling worked
into four stems. A child's toy inside
says "Moo" when the basket is
turned over. *Photo, Lee Erlin
Snow.*

BASKET WITH FEATHERS. Carol
Shaw. Twined basket with a coiled
lid. Hand-dyed sisal and linen.
Photo, Lee Erlin Snow.

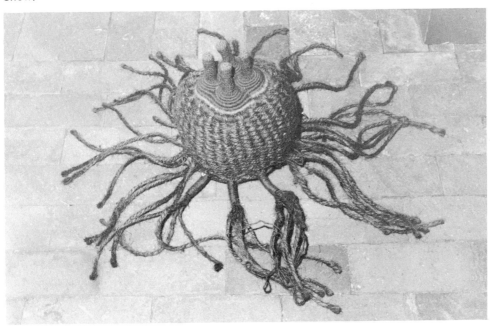

WALL HANGING. Larry Peterson. 9 feet high. A sisal wall hanging combines twining and wrapping in the basket technique. *Courtesy, Artist.*

HANGING FETISH BASKET. Virginia H. Barber. A hanging basket form as sculpture using two assembled coiled sections. Jute foundation is wrapped with sisal, wool, and synthetic fibers. The lid buttons onto the container with six large black wooden beads. Feathers, beads, and fish vertebrae are added at bottom. *Courtesy, Artist.*

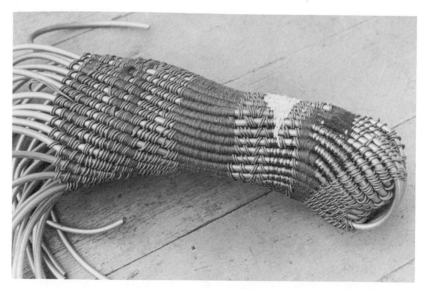

FLOOR SCULPTURE. Suellen Glashausser. Jute and plastic twined and woven around plastic tubing used as warp. *Courtesy, Artist.*

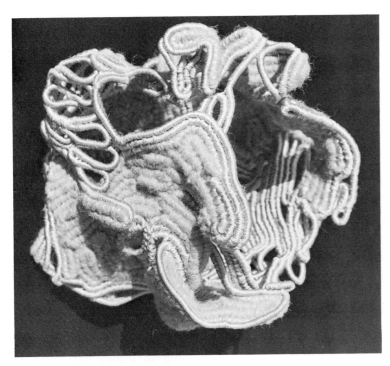

FREE-FORM BASKET. Joan Austin. Basket coiling is used to create an abstract shape. Shiny and dull threads are used for contrast.

CARROT. Carol Shaw. Twining is begun from the tip, and warps are added to expand the shape. Warp ends are used for the wrapped and unraveled "greenery" at top. *Photo (taken at the Laguna Beach Art Museum), Lee Erlin Snow.*

NEW VIRGIN VILLAGE. Dorothy Riley. Twining, weaving, and wrapping. *Photo (taken at the Laguna Beach Art Museum). Lee Erlin Snow.*

181

14 Potpourri of Additional Ideas

When gathering materials for a book like this, it is inevitable that many submitted pieces do not fall easily into specific chapter categories. It would be ridiculous to omit them simply because they defy classification. These pieces have been included specifically because they can inspire and motivate the reader in a multitude of creative ways.

The following examples are combinations of many techniques and materials. They include works used for clothing and body adornment, for furniture, and for other purposes.

Many knitted examples submitted showed innovative strides, but there were not enough exciting new directions to warrant an entire chapter. Examples of some knitted pieces by Helen Richards and Ted Hallman illustrate the artist's ability to employ knitting for expressive statements and may inspire the knitter to create pieces entirely of knitting or to combine knitting with the techniques demonstrated elsewhere.

Jewelry examples shown here and in Chapter 6 illustrate effective combinations with metals, bones, beads, and other materials. Many of the smaller "wall hangings" are pinned to dress fronts and used as jewelry or dress ornamentation for special occasions. Small, lightweight woven pieces are especially suitable for hanging from jewelry findings, lightweight wire, plastic rods, or small pieces of decorative wood. So plan your weavings to do double duty—from wall to wear.

PRIMITIVE SHIELD. Gervaise Livingston. 9 feet high, 5 feet wide. Woven and rewoven fabric using wool, yak hair, alpaca, Peruvian handspun, jute, and turkey feathers. *Photo, Morton Witz. Collection, Shirley Johnston.*

EXPERIMENTAL FABRIC. Sandra Koerlin. 13 inches high, 18 inches wide. A simple statement using a wood crate as the frame and part of the final presentation. Cotton and silk fiber. *Courtesy, Artist.*

TAPESTRY: GRAY, BLACK, AND WHITE. Elfleda Russell. 5-1/2 feet high, 4 feet wide. Handspun natural wool worked on a large frame using weaving and macramé. The purpose was to oppose three-dimensional macramé with the crisp vertical and horizontal lines of weaving. The macramé strings were slip knotted onto warps, and the procedure involved alternating between knotting and weaving. *Collection, Graham Gavel*

VIRILITY. Ruby Mielke. Weaving on heavy jute warp with driftwood and bones. Ends have been unraveled. *Collection, Mr. and Mrs. Herbert Snow, Los Angeles.*

GRAY WALL HANGING. Susan Lyttle. 6 feet high. Braids, wrapped threads, and knotless netting using partially spun roving and yarn for a thick, lumpy, accentuated texture. *Courtesy, Artist.*

HANGING. Janet Kuemmerlein. 10 feet high. Double weave with free float warps and sticks added. The textured section is rya knotting. *Photo, L. D. Jones.*

185

BODY ORNAMENT. Merle H. Sykora. Chased pewter pieces were subtly molded to fit the body. They were fastened (the front is similar to the back), placed on a padded hanger, and threaded with yarn. The yarn was knotted to create the cascade. *Courtesy, Artist.*

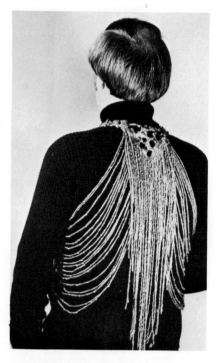

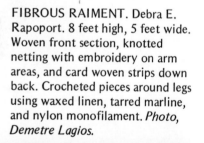

FIBROUS RAIMENT. Debra E. Rapoport. 8 feet high, 5 feet wide. Woven front section, knotted netting with embroidery on arm areas, and card woven strips down back. Crocheted pieces around legs using waxed linen, tarred marline, and nylon monofilament. *Photo, Demetre Lagios.*

FIBROUS RAIMENT. Debra E. Rapoport. Woven triangles and a macramé collar were made on a handmade triangle frame, which would yield three selvages. Each triangle assembled is about 6 inches wide. Linen, silk, wool, cotton, and rayon yarns were used. *Photo, Demetre Lagios.*

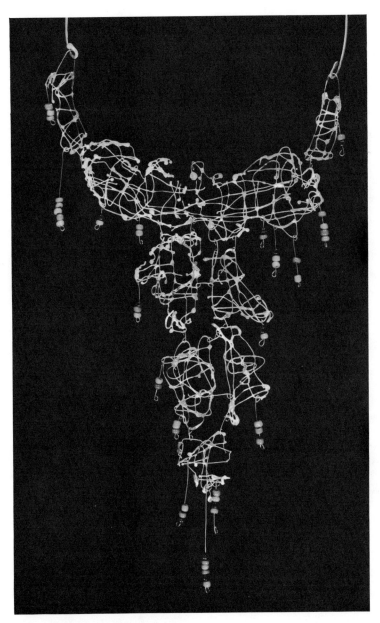

WOVEN NECKLACE. Susan B.
Hickam. 14 inches high, 7 inches
wide. Sterling silver woven on 12
warps using a frame loom. After
weaving was completed, the silver
was fused, forged, cut into shapes,
and reassembled. Glass beads were
added. *Courtesy, Artist.*

SUMMER AND WINTER. Verda
Elliott. 16 inches long, 8 inches
wide. Coiling sewn to weaving.

CHESS SET AND BOARD. Susie
Henzie. Hand-woven chess pieces
are shaped over Styrofoam cones.
Frame-woven chessboard.

FRANNY. Sharon La Pierre. 15 inches high, 12 inches wide, 4 inches deep. Tapestry pillow made on a frame loom using wool, horsehair, velvet cording, and solid brass rings. *Courtesy, Artist.*

PEE WEE. Sharon La Pierre. 11 inches high, 11 inches wide, 10 inches deep. Raw silk, camel's hair, wool, raffia. *Collection, Wilcke Smith.*

CHAIR. Bucky King. Chair
fashioned from copper bathroom
pipes. Pipes were warped so that
the back and seat could be woven
with colored jute. *Courtesy, Artist.*

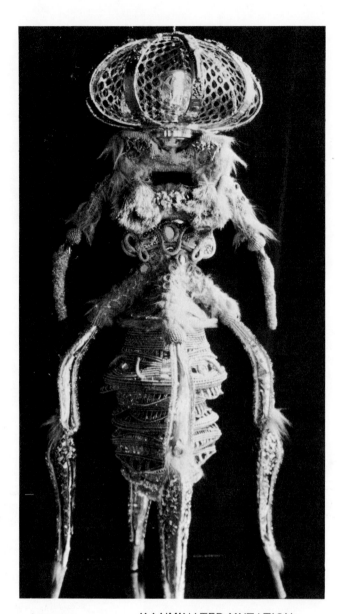

ILLUMINATED MUTATION.
Stephen D. Thurston. 60 inches
high, 26 inches in diameter. A
woven form that serves as a floor
lamp utilizes silver metallic yarn,
braided cords, imitation fur, mylar,
fabric, leather, rattail, chrome
strips, metallic chenille, mirrors,
nickel-plated studs, and chrome
lamp fixtures. All materials are
silver. Methods include loom-woven
tapestry and rya, frame-woven
bands, crochet, appliqué, stitchery,
and macramé. *Courtesy, Artist.*

FOOT ENCLOSURE. Debra E. Rapoport. 3 feet high, 2-1/2 feet wide, 2 feet deep. Constructed in pieces and arranged into a structural form using twining and wrapping. Materials are cotton batting, terry cloth, printed textiles, and mixed yarns. *Photo, Demetre Lagios.*

BODY COVERING. Debra E. Rapoport. 4-1/2 feet high, 2 feet wide. Plastic berry baskets and crushed plastic strips are the substructure for the macramé surface of various plastic cords and mixed yarns. *Photo, Demetre Lagios.*

191

MENEHUNE. Susana Rolando.
Spain. 66 feet long, 66 feet wide.
Floating and solidly woven areas
are magnificently draped and
developed to utilize negative and
positive space in a two-dimensional
presentation. *Courtesy, the Egg and
the Eye Gallery, Los Angeles.*

TARANTULA. Helen Barbarek. 5
feet high, 3 feet wide. An unusual
treatment. Floating warps in a
repeat pattern are combined with
feathers and beads. *Courtesy,
Artist.*

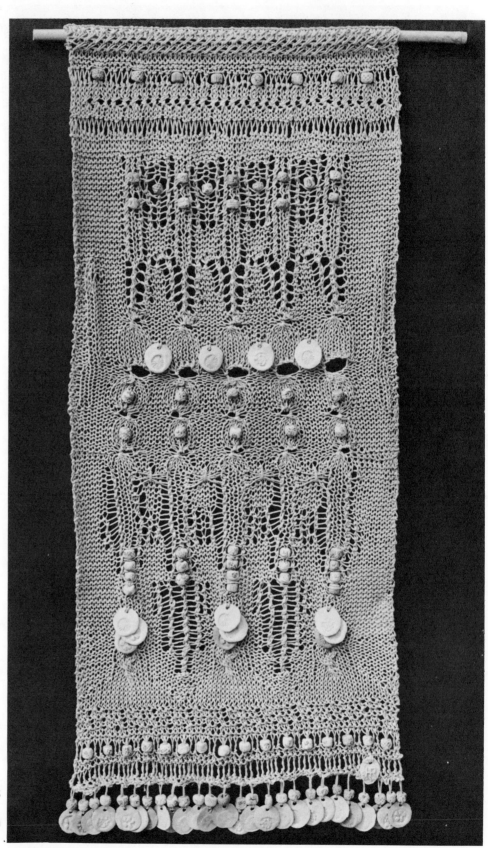

SANDSTONE. Helen Richards. 48 inches high, 20 inches wide. A knitted panel in natural color yarn with ceramic beads.

ALBE'S TREE. Ted Hallman. 9 feet high. Knitting with cotton on steel rings. *Courtesy, Artist.*

⊓Information Center

Supply Sources

The following supply sources are listed for your convenience. Materials offered and charges for samples and catalogs are subject to change without notice. No endorsement or responsibility is implied by the authors.

Dick Blick
P.O. Box 1267
Galesburg, Ill. 61401
  Supplies; yarns, beads, basketry, books.

Cane & Basket Supply Co.
1283 S. Cochran Ave.
Los Angeles, Calif. 90019
  Reed, seagrass, raffia, books on basketry.

Carmel Valley Weavers Supply
Box 77A Route 1 or
1342 Camino Del Mar
Del Mar, Calif. 92014
  Spindles, cords, fleece, dyes, yarns. Imported handspun yarns, general weaving and spinning supplies, basket materials, beads, books. Samples: $.50 Loom catalog: $.50.

Casa de las Tejedoras
1619 East Edinger
Santa Ana, Calif. 92705
  Fibers, equipment, fleece, spinning supplies, beads, books.

Craft Kaleidoscope
6412 Ferguson St.
Indianapolis, Ind. 46220
  Handspun and imported yarns, supplies, beads, books.

Craft Yarns of R.I.
603 Mineral Spring Ave.
Pawtucket, R.I. 02862
  Yarns, jute, accessories for weaving. Samples: $.50.

Creative Hand Weavers
3824 Sunset Blvd.
Los Angeles, Calif. 90026
  Fleece, imported handspun yarns, artificial silk, unusual novelty yarns and varieties, thick colored jute. Samples and catalog: $.50.

Dharma Trading Co.
P.O. Box 1288
Berkeley, Calif. 94701
  Fleece, handspun wools, imported yarns, supplies, dyes, books. Samples and catalog: $.50.

Frederick J. Fawcett, Inc.
129 South Street
Boston, Mass. 02111
  Assorted linen yarns, some worsted. Samples: $1.00.

Gettinger Feather Co.
38 W. 38th St.
New York, N.Y. 10018
  Natural feathers, raw and dyed. Sample package: $1.50.

Gillian's Specialties
P.O. Box 633
Solana Beach, Calif. 92075
  Hand-carved wood weavers' tools, combs, battens, pickup sticks, shuttles in select and exotic woods.

Hollywood Fancy Feather Co.
512 S. Broadway
Los Angeles, Calif. 90013
  Assorted feathers — minimum order: $10.00.

International Handcraft & Supply
103 Lyndon St.
Hermosa Beach, Calif. 90254
 Fleece, handspun, imported yarns, raw silk, basketry supplies, beads, books, weaving and spinning supplies. Samples: $1.00, returnable on first purchase. Minimum order: $5.00.

Sachiye Jones
2050 Friendly
Euguene, Ore. 97405
 Handspun and hand-dyed fleece and yarns.

Lamb's End
16861 Hamilton Ave.
Highland Park, Mich. 48203
 Weaving and spinning supplies, fleece, assorted yarns. Catalog: $2.50, deductible from first order.

Lily Mills Co.
Dept. HWH
Shelby, N.C. 28150
 Assorted yarns, jutes, threads and weaving supplies. Swatch card showing all samples: $.50. In-dividual sample cards: $.25 each.

Loomloft Designs Ltd.
300 King St., East
Toronto 29, Ontario, Canada
 Wool, linen and special yarns. Samples: $.50.

Macramé & Weaving Supply
63 East Adams St.
Chicago, Ill. 60603
 Assorted yarns and cords, buckles, and beads. Catalog $.50 deduc-tible from first order.

Jeanne Malsada
Box 28182
Atlanta, Georgia 30328
 Yarns, beads.

The Mannings
R. D. 2
East Berlin, Pa. 17316
 Yarns, all spinning and weaving supplies, beads, books. Samples and catalog: $.50.

Northwest Handcraft House
110 West Esplanade
North Vancouver, B.C., Canada
 All weaving supplies, spinning supplies, imported wools, jute, flax, cotton, etc., natural and

synthetic dyes, books. Catalog: $.50. Sample cards $2.00 -set of 10 or $.25 per card.

Pauline Patton
134 Edgecumbe Rd.
Tauranga, New Zealand
 Fleece and handspun wool, natural, vegetable and chemically dyed.

The Pendleton Shop
Box 233 - Jordan Road
Sedona, Arizona 86336
 Assorted yarns, Navaho handspun wool and mohair, supplies, books.

Charlotte Potts Weaving Studio
511 Calle Arroyo
One Thousand Oaks, Calif. 91360
 Imported yarns. Samples: $.50.

Helen Richards
1479 Glenneyre
Laguna Beach, Calif. 92651

Robin & Russ Handweavers
533 N. Adams St.
McMinnville, Ore. 97128
 Large variety of yarns, fibers, weaving supplies, lace bobbins, books.

Schact Spindle Co.
656 Pleasant St.
Boulder, Colorado 80302
 Spindles, rope machine, looms, beaters, misc. supplies.

Tahki Imports
336 West End Ave.
New York, N.Y. 10023
 Wild yarns, handspun wools. Samples: $.75.

Osma Gallinger Tod
319 Mendoza Ave.
Coral Gables, Fla. 33134
 Bobbins and lacemaking supplies, weaving materials, books.

Warp, Woof & Potpourri
514 N. Lake Ave.
Pasadena, Calif. 91104
 Assorted weaver's supplies: yarns, beads, feathers, boards, spindles, dyes.

The Weavers Loft
320 Blue Bell Road
Williamstown, N.J. 08094
 Assorted weaving yarns and sup-plies, leather lacing, beads, twine spinning supplies, books.

The Yarn Depot, Inc.
545 Sutter St.
San Francisco, Calif. 94102
Assorted yarns, beads, supplies,
books. Sample cards: $.50 to
$1.50. Bimonthly samples club.

The Yarn Merchant
8533 Beveraly Blvd.
Los Angeles, Calif. 90048
Imported handspun wool and
linen, supplies, beads, feathers,
weaving boards.

Book Dealers Specializing in Art & Crafts

The Book Barn
P. O. Box 256
Avon, Conn. 06268
Catalog: $.50.

Craft & Hobby Book Service
P.O. Box 626
Pacific Grove, Calif. 93950
Catalog with supplier's list: $1.00

K. R. Drummond, Bookseller
Hart Grove
Ealing Common
London, W 5, England

Museum Books, Inc.
48 E. 43rd St.
New York, N.Y. 10017

The Unicorn
P.O. Box 645
Rockville, Md. 20851

Periodicals of Special Interest

Artisan Crafts
P.O. Box 548
Maitland, Fla. 32751
Quarterly

Craft Horizons
American Craftsmen's Council
44 W. 53rd St.
New York, N.Y. 10019
Bimonthly

Handweaver & Craftsman
220 Fifth Ave.
New York, N.Y. 10001
Quarterly

Quarterly Journal of the Guilds of
Weavers, Spinners & Dyers
1 Harrington Road
Brighton 6, England

The Shuttle Service
319 Mendoza Ave.
Coral Gables, Fla. 33134
Bimonthly

Shuttle, Spindle & Dye-pot
(with membership to Hand-
weavers Guild of America)
339 North Steele Rd.
West Hartford, Conn. 06117
Quarterly

Warp & Weft
533 N. Adams St.
McMinnville, Ore. 97128
10 issues a year

⌐ Selected Bibliography

Atwater, Mary Meigs. *Byways in Handweaving*. New York: Macmillan, 1954.

Blumenau, Lili. *Creative Design in Wall Hanging*. New York: Crown, 1967.

Dendel, Esther Warner. *Needleweaving . . . Easy as Embroidery*. New York: Doubleday, 1972.

de Dillmont, Theresa. *Encyclopedia of Needlework*. France: Mulhouse.

Harvey, Virginia I., and Tidball, Harriet. *Weft Twining*. Lansing, Michigan: Shuttle Craft Guild, 1969.

Hastie, Reid, and Schmidt, Christian. *Encounter with Art*. New York: McGraw Hill, 1969.

Hickethier, Alfred. *Color Mixing by Number*. New York: Van Nostrand Reinhold, 1970.

Hosking, Phyllis. *Basket Making for Amateurs*. London: G. Bell and Sons, 1960.

_____. *Indian Basket Weaving*. New York: Dover, 1971.

Lesch, Alma. *Vegetable Dyeing*. New York: Watson-Guptill, 1970.

Lyford, Carrie A. *Ojibwa Crafts*. Lawrence, Kansas: U.S. Department of the Interior, Bureau of Indian Affairs, 1943.

Meilach, Dona Z. *Creating Art from Fibers and Fabrics*. Chicago: Regnery, 1972.

Meilach, Dona Z. *Contemporary Batik and Tie-Dye*. New York: Crown, 1973 (Chapter 14 on Synthetic Dyes).

Meilach, Dona Z. *Macramé: Creative Design in Knotting*. New York: Crown, 1971.

Rainey, Sarita R. *Weaving Without a Loom*. Worcester, Mass.: Davis, 1969.

Regensteiner, Else. *The Art of Weaving*. New York: Van Nostrand Reinhold, 1970.

Robinson, Stuart. *A History of Dyed Textiles*. Great Britain: Studio Vista, Ltd. and Cambridge: M.I.T. Press, 1969.

Whiteford, Andrew Hunter. *North American Indian Arts*. New York: Golden, 1970.

Wilson, Jean. *Weaving Is for Anyone*. New York: Van Nostrand Reinhold, 1967.

⌐Index

C.P. = color photo. See pages between pages 90 and 91.

Abakanowicz, Magdalena, 106, C.P.
Ahrens, Earlene, 6, 66, 75, 76
Amaral, Olga de, 112
Animal fibers, 10, 12
Armatures, 78, 160
Austin, Joan, 181

Barbarek, Helen, 193
Barber, Virginia H., 99, 177, 180
Basketmaking, 4, 5, 9, 34, 174-181
Bath, Virginia, 132, 133
Baughn, Mary, 116, 117
Beads in endings, 41
Beater, 20, 21
Beating, 22
Bergstrom, Annabel, 70
Bernard, Eileen, 76, 92
Bernstein, Liz, 91
Beutlich, Tadek, 10-11
Black, Virginia, 9, 35
Boards, 48-65
Bobbin lace, 122-130
Bohnenkamp, Leslie G., 121
Borlund, Linda, 18, 87, 93
Braiding, 4
   in lacemaking, 126-127
   Mexican double, 120
   Osage, 4, 114, 118, 119, 121
Branches, weaving on, 8, 96
Brandford, Joanne, 148-150
Brooks Bouquet, 31
Brown, Susan H., 170, C.P.
Buic, Jagoda, 107

Cardboard, weaving on, 66-77
Carding, 135
Carstenson, Blanche, 173
Chapman, Barbara Waszak, 105
Chapman, Jane, 94
Childress, Marianne, 94, 105
Circular forms, 69, 78-99
Clothing
   woven, 66, 67, 72-73, 76, 151, 172,
      186, 191
Coat hangers, weaving on, 78, 90, 97
Coiling, 4, 9, 176
Coleman, Stana, 58, 88
Collars, woven, 70-71
Color wheel, 17
Colors, 4
   alternating, 31
   changes, directions of, 27
   changes, techniques for creating, 26-27
   combining, 17
   schemes, planning, 15, 45 ·

Constantine, Lois, 5
Cook, Sherry, 167
Cotton, 12, 15
Coutts, Lucele, 9, 177
Crochet, 4, 9, 156-173
Cylinder, weaving on, 83
Cyr, Stephanie, 19

Designs, ideas for, 32, 33, 44-47, 82,
Dickerhoff, Betty, 75
Dolls, woven, 59
Double crochet, 158
Double weave, 50, 51, 60, 84
Dovetailing, 26, 27
Dyeing, 15-16, 135

Egyptian knot, 28
Elliott, Verda, 187
Endings, 36, 39, 69
   ideas for, 4, 38, 41, 44
   tassels, 40
   wrapped, 36-37

Fangon, Dolores, 164
Fibers, 2, 10-19
   for basketmaking, 4
   combinations, 2, 18
   for lacemaking, 124
   samples, 10, 13, 15
Finger crochet, 159
Finger weaving, 4, 114-121
Fink, Shirley, 92, 102, 113
Fleece, 10, 15, 134, 135
Found objects, 8, 78, 92
Frames, 48-65
   knotless netting on, 146-148
   large, made of two frames, 62
   notching, 48, 50
   portable, 63
   ready-to-use, Lilette, 62
   warping, 50, 63
Frederick, Deborah, 90
Free-form shapes, 32, 45. 77, 89 *see also*
   Sculptural forms

Ghiordes knots, 4, 29, 32, 33
Ginsberg, Ruth, 30
Glashausser, Suellen, 18, 119, 120
Gulick, Evelyn M., 155

Hall, Phyllis, 40, 74, 86
Hallman, Ted, 182, 195, C.P.
Hanging sculptures, 103
Hangings, see Wall hangings
Headings, 36
Heddles, 48, 63

Hemp, 13
Hennessey, Helen, 71
Henzie, Susie, 188
Herringbone, 33
Heyden, Sylvia, C.P.
Hickam, Susan B., 187
Hicks, Sheila, 109
Holmer, Martie, 173
Hoops, 78-99
    attaching crochet to, 160
    knotless netting on, 150
Houston, Anita, C.P.

Interlocking, 27

Jacobs, Ferne, C.P.
Jaunsem, Sharon, 26, 29, 39
Jewelry, 128, 182, 186, 187
Jones, Frances F., 82
Jones, Mary L., C.P.
Jute, 12, 13, 15

King, Bucky, 172, 190
Kleinberg, Judith I., 153, 172
Knight, Jane, 9, 168, 169, 170
Knitting, 182, 194-195
Knitting rake, 67, 88
Knotless netting, 4, 140-155
Knots
    Egyptian, 28
    ghiordes, 4, 29, 32, 33
    overhand, 41
    rya, 4, 9, 26, 29, 32
    square, 38, 41
    texture, 28-29
Koerlin, Sandra, 6, 184
Krythe, Tina, 87, 146-147
Kuemmerlein, Janet, 185

Lacemaking, 4, 122-133
Lamp, floor, 190
La Pierre, Sharon, 77, 189
Lehman, Susan, 170
Leno weave, 30
Lilette frame, 62
Livingston, Gervaise, 182-183
Looms
    frame, from beach chair back, 58
    Todd, 58
Lott, Gwynne, 120
Lyttle, Susan, 58, 168, 185

McAfee, Phoebe, 154-155
McNinch, Janet, 144-145, 153
Macramé, 4
Malec, Kathy, 34
Masks, 99, 120, 170
Masonite circles, 80-81
Materials
    for off-loom weaving, 6, 7, 20-21
    for weaving on cardboard, 67
    see also Fibers; Yarns
Meilach, Dona, 176
Mexican double braiding, 120
Mielke, Ruby, 184
Miller, Bea, 154-155

Miller, Fern, 165
Minkowitz, Norma C., 171
Monochromatic color schemes, 17

Nagano, Momo, 2-3, 8, 27, 59-61, 66,
    78-79, 84, 96, C.P.
Necklaces, 99, 128, 187
Needle
    lace, 124
    looping, 147
    for weaving weft, 20, 21
    wrapping with, 36
Netting, knotless, 4, 140-155
Nottingham, Walter, 18, 100-101, 166,
    169

Obye, Pat, 33, C.P.
Open weaves, 30-31
Osage braiding, 4, 114, 118, 119, 121
Over two, under two weave, 33
Overhand knot, 41

Paper, use in weaving, 7
Patterns, 20-28
    double-weave, 33
    free-form shapes, 32
    ideas for, 32, 33, 44-47, 82, 128, 144,
        151-152, 164, 165
    in lace, creating, 127, 128
    leno, 30
    open-weave, 30-31
    plain-weave, 4, 22, 24, 25
    tabby, 4, 22, 24, 25
    twill, 33
Peruvian wrap, 37
Peterson, Larry, 180
Pillows
    for lacemaking, 122, 124, 125
    weaving sewn on, 77
    woven, 58, 81, 189
Plain weave, 4, 22, 24, 25
Platus, Libby, 65
Plies, 4, 13
    multiple, working yarn into, 5
    twisting, 138-139
Potter, Carolyn, 98
Pullover, 76
Purses, 74-75

Rapoport, Debra E., 186, 191
Rayon, 12
Richards, Helen, 171, 182, 194
Richards, Joyce, 45, 48-49, 64, 104, C.P.
Riley, Dorothy, 18, 93, 108, 110-111,
    181
Rings, weaving on, 82
Rodwell, Marianne, 30, 88
Rolando, Susana, 192-193
Room divider, woven, 65
Rope-making machine, 138-139
Roth, Winifred, 95
Round lace weavings, 129, 133
Roving, 10, 137
Rug beater, weaving on, 92
Russell, Elfleda, 97, 184
Rya, 4, 9, 26, 29, 32

Saks, Joyce, 95
Sampler
    lacemaking, 122-123
    weaving, 20, 22-23
Sashes, braided, 119
Saylor, Melicent, 75
Schacht rope-making machine, 138-139
Schawcroft, Barbara, 140-141
Sculptural forms, 5, 65, 100-113, 130,
    153-155, 161-165, 168, 170, 172,
    180, 184, 190, 191, 195
Shaw, Carol, 179, 181
Shed, 23, 117
Shed sticks, 23, 50, 62
Shubin, Nadine, 28
Shuttle, 63
Siewert-Miller, Elisabet, 167
Singerman, Jean, 104
Single crochet, 158
Single weave, 51
Sisal, 12, 13, 15
Sketches, 40, 42
Slit tapestry weave, 26
Snow, Lee Erlin, 7, 25, 32, 37, 40, 52,
    53, 56, 58, 69, 70, 77, 87, 93, 96,
    105, 124, 161-163, 176, 178, 179,
    181, C.P.
Solari, Mieke, 51
Soumak, 28
Spanish lace, 31
Spindle, 135
Spinning, 5, 134-139
Square knot, 38
Sulentor, Sharon, 113
Swenson, Pat, 89
Sykora, Merle H., 186
Sylvester, Audrey V., 156-157
Synthetic fibers, 12

Tabby, 4, 22, 24, 25
Tablecloth, 144-145
Tassels, 40
Teasing fleece, 135
Tension sticks, 63
Thurston, Stephen D., 190
Todd loom, 58
Tokushige, Emiko, 103
Triple crochet, 159
Tubes, weaving on, 83
Tubular weaving, 50, 51
Twigs, use in weaving, 5, 7
Twill weave, 4, 33
Twining, 4, 34, 174, 178

Under two, over two, 24, 25
Underwood, Martha, 5, 19, 36, 40, 42,
    46-47

Van Gelder, Lydia, 125, 128, 129-130
Vegetable fibers, 12

Ventre, Mary, 172

Wall hangings, 9, 13, 26, 34, 35, 42,
    48-49, 51, 56-58, 60-61, 64, 80, 81,
    82, 84-87, 93, 94, 96, 97, 114-117,
    119, 121, 124, 131-133, 166-170,
    172, 173, 180, 184-185, 192-194
Ward, Evelyn Svec, 131
Warp end bars, 63
Warps, 20, 21
    holding in position, 48
    separating, 23, 48, 50
    wrapping, 33
Waters, Marie, 174-175
Weaves
    density, 50
    double, 50, 51, 60, 84
    leno, 30
    open, 30-31
    plain, 4, 22, 24, 25
    single, 51
    tabby, 4, 22, 24, 25
    twill, 33
Weaving
    estimating quantities of yarn needed,
        13-14
    finger, 4, 114-121
    finishing, 55, 69
    frames and boards, 48-65
    larger than height of frame, 48
    materials for, 6, 7, 20-21, 67
    room-size, 65
    tubular, 50, 51
Weber, Frances C., 62, 81, 83, 85
Wefts, 21
    in fingerweaving, 116, 118
    needle for weaving, 20, 21
    in Osage braiding, 118
    threads, woven in, 55
    two worked at once, 21, 34
    working in patterns, 55
Wittenberg, Barbara, 84, 114-115, 119
Wood, weaving on, 5, 6, 7
Woof, 20
Wool, 10, 12, 15
Wrapping, 4
    with a needle, 36
    Peruvian wrap, 37
    warp, 33

Yardage, converting to weight, 14
Yarns
    for crochet, 156
    dyeing, 15-16, 135
    estimating quantities needed, 13-14
    ply, 4, 13, 138-139
    spinning, 5, 134-139
    varieties, 12-13
    working into multiple plies, 5

Zeisler, Claire, 108